CULINARY TREASURES OF JAPAN

John Belleme
Jan Belleme

AVERY PUBLISHING GROUP INC.
Garden City Park, New York

Cover Design: Akiko Aoyagi Shurtleff
In-House Editor: Marie Caratozzolo
Typesetter: Bonnie Freid
Original Artwork: Akiko Aoyagi Shurtleff

Library of Congress Cataloging-in-Publication Data

Belleme, John.
    Culinary Treasures of Japan : the art of making and using traditional Japanese foods / John Belleme
and Jan Belleme.
        p.   cm.
    Includes index.
    ISBN 0-89529-509-1

    1. Cookery, Japanese. 2. Cookery—Japan. I. Belleme, Jan.   II. Title.

TX724.5.J3B453 1992   92-17982
641.5952—dc20   CIP

Printed in the United States of America

10 9 8 7 6 5 4 3 2

Contents

This book is dedicated to
Akiyoshi Kazama
in appreciation for his great spirit
and determination

Acknowledgments

We would especially like to thank Akiyoshi Kazama, founder and president of Mitoku, for his commitment to the highest standards of quality, not only with respect to whole organic ingredients and the delicious, authentic taste of Japan, but for the precise details of making these wholesome traditional foods as well. For over twenty-five years, Mr. Kazama has tirelessly searched the Japanese countryside for those few remaining Japanese food producers who could meet the strict standards of the world macrobiotic movement.

We would also like to thank the staff of Mitoku for their efforts in the worldwide distribution of these quality foods, and for their help in the preparation of this book by answering questions and translating specific information about traditional food manufacturing. Much credit for the book and, indeed, the day to day running of Mitoku goes to Christopher Dawson, international sales and product development director. Since 1979, Dawson has gained vast experience by working closely with the skilled men and women who make Mitoku products, as well as with Mitoku's many distributors around the world. We have been inspired by his dedication to keeping alive Japanese traditional food heritage. Our thanks to staff members Tomoo Abe and Toyofumi Yoshida.

Others who have aided Mr. Kazama in the running of Mitoku over the years include Blake Rankin and Terrie Adams of the United States, Ferro Ledvinka of Italy, Michelle Harboun of France, and Robbie Swinnerton of England. A special thanks to Robbie Swinnerton for doing some of the original research used in this book.

In addition to Mitoku, we are grateful to all traditional Japanese food makers who are upholding the highest standards of quality in the face of stiff competition from companies using quicker, cheaper mass-production methods. Their integrity and great concern for individual and environmental health are rare in present-day food processing.

We appreciate the efforts of other Japanese foods exporters, as well as international natural foods distributors who have made it their business to track down the finest traditional foods and make them available in their regions of the world.

Several individuals have contributed tremendously to the awareness of the value of these foods, thereby creating the demand that supports and completes the link from manufacturer to consumer. This list is by no means complete, but certainly the following people have played a major role: George and Lima Ohsawa, Michio and Aveline Kushi, Herman and Cornelia Aihara, Noboru Muramoto, and William and Akiko Aoyagi Shurtleff. It was the Shurtleffs' many books about Japanese foods that inspired us to go to Japan, and it was Akiko's beautiful illustrations in this book that gave us the encouragement to complete our task.

We would also like to thank long-time friend Sandy Pukel. Sandy introduced John to macrobiotics in 1974. For over twenty years, as the founder of the Oak Feed Store in Miami and the Macrobiotic Foundation of Florida, Sandy has created numerous opportunities for us and thousands of others for a healthier way of life.

We would also like to thank all those on the staff of Avery Publishing Group, especially publisher Rudy Shur, and Marie Caratozzolo, our editor, for her encouragement and editorial expertise.

Foreword

After witnessing the needless human sacrifice and the decimation of Europe, Asia, and the South Pacific Islands during World War II, I became a World Federalist. I continuously sought ways and solutions for establishing peace on our planet. I studied the teachings of many prominent scientists, philosophers, educators, and religious leaders.

It seemed, however, the more I learned about political and social structures, the more I became aware of their ineffectiveness. How, I wondered, can humanity evolve unless the biological, psychological, and spiritual quality of the human race also evolve? It soon became clear to me that humanity is shaped by two major factors: the environment, and dietary habits and patterns. Peace and war, health and sickness, happiness and unhappiness, and all human affairs have roots, origins, and causes that can be traced back to diet and environment. Of these two elements, however, diet is the one to which we can apply the exercise of our free will and human consciousness on a daily basis.

I studied various dietary patterns of different cultures and reflected upon the numerous positive and negative events that have occurred throughout history. I concluded that within the natural order of the universe, to which human beings belong, there is an ideal diet that is most suitable for the highest development of humans. The principles of the ideal diet are briefly summarized as follows:

- Dietary practices must be adaptable to (and suitable for) one's natural environment.

- For those living in temperate, subtropical, and tropical regions, whole grains should be consumed daily as the principal food, supplemented by a variety of vegetables, beans and bean products, sea vegetables, fruits, seeds, and nuts. Animal-food consumption should be occasional and should not exceed 5 to 20 percent of daily meals.

- All foods should be organically grown, naturally processed, and properly prepared.

In 1959, my wife Aveline and I took the first step in supplying ideal dietary foods to people living in the United States. We established Erewhon, a small store in Boston, Massachusetts, which Aveline ran. We began to distribute brown rice, whole wheat, beans, and a few other products to a small number of customers. We knew that other indispensible food products were necessary for ideal dietary consumption, but finding suppliers was not an easy task.

Erewhon needed to offer foods that were naturally produced, processed, and prepared. It was important for Erewhon to supply good-quality natural sea vegetables and healthy traditional beverages, as well as condiments and natural sweeteners. In the course of my search for suppliers, I was introduced to Mr. Akiyoshi Kazama of Mitoku Company, Ltd. in Tokyo. It was not long before I realized that I had found the one person with whom I could share my dream of a healthy, happy, peaceful human race on this planet.

Aveline and I requested high standards of food quality. Mr. Kazama immediately understood what we wanted and accepted our strict conditions wholeheartedly. He began his search for food producers and manufacturers who were sincere and willing to supply the kind of quality products that we requested. In 1968, Mr. Kazama's first shipment to the Erewhon Company consisted of $3,000 worth of high-quality Japanese foods. For twenty-five years, his collaboration continued unfailingly. Although many requests and demands were made upon Mr. Kazama and Mitoku Company, he always did his best to deliver food products of the highest quality.

We have never had the slightest hesitation in introducing Mr. and Mrs. Kazama and the Mitoku staff to natural foods importers, distributors, retailers, and consumers. Our trust is complete. Again and again we recommend their products, not only because of Mitoku Company's high standards, but because of their implementation of the best shipping methods. The name Mitoku represents a guarantee of quality for Mr. Kazama's customers worldwide. Approximately 40 percent of Mitoku's shipments currently go to the United States, 40 percent go to Europe, and 20 percent to Australia and New Zealand. Mitoku's contributions to the natural foods market have played a major role and have been a decisive factor in the revolution of Western dietary habits.

As the Mitoku Company developed its international operations, Mr. and Mrs. Kazama often assisted students from Western countries, inviting them to Japan and arranging unique opportunities for them to become directly involved in the preparation of traditional natural foods. Mitoku hired young people who wanted to gain this unique experience. Needless to say, many seized the opportunity that had been gracefully offered to them.

The authors of this book, John and Jan Belleme, are two Americans who benefited from Mr. Kazama's generous help. Upon our recommendation, Mr. Kazama made the necessary contacts and arrangements with Onazaki, a traditional miso-making company located north of Tokyo. John and Jan were able to study first-hand the age-old tradition of miso processing. After returning to America, John and Jan, along with a small group of investors, originated the American Miso Company in North Carolina.

Christopher Geoffrey Dawson, a native New Zealander, also seized the opportunity to learn from Mr. and Mrs. Kazama. Dawson joined Mitoku in 1979 and is still working as a much-valued staff member with important responsibilities in the development of new markets and organic product lines all over the world. He has gained expertise in both the Japanese language, as well as in the knowledge of organic and macrobiotic food-quality development and marketing.

The various food producers and manufacturers with whom Mr. Kazama established close relationships supply natural macrobiotic-quality food products to many different countries. All of these suppliers are sincere and competent people who are committed to producing the best possible quality of food. Through a process of tireless discussions and negotiations, Mitoku has enlisted the help and participation of hundreds of companies, producers, and manufacturers. Some of these companies are small single-family industries, while others operate on a larger scale.

From its initial $3,000 shipment in 1968, Mitoku has traveled a long and rewarding journey over the past twenty-five years. Its customers and affiliated companies can now be found in almost thirty-five countries throughout the world. We are immensely grateful to these companies that share the dream and vision of human health and world peace. Together with the farmers and manufacturers, they are the true pioneers of the natural food movement.

Food serves a fundamental function in the establishment of peace in society. Organic macrobiotic-quality food is the tool that can ensure the realization of this peaceful revolution of true health and social well-being throughout the world. Such is the essence of the macrobiotic teachings that my wife and I, together with many other teachers, have been spreading throughout the planet.

For the past ten years, Mitoku Company has echoed and supported the macrobiotic perspective with its motto "Ishoku-Dogen," which can be translated as "Food is Medicine." This saying has been part of the Oriental heritage of wisdom that has been transmitted from generation to generation for thousands of years. Food is medicine. Without the daily consumption of proper food, health eventually declines, and physical and psychological symptoms inevitably appear. Without the deep understanding that food is medicine, that food is the source of life itself, the human race will eventually disappear from the planet through sickness, war, environmental pollution, and all the other illnesses that presently plague society. With the motto "Ishoku Dogen," Mitoku silently but strongly promotes the best available food and medicine to millions of people.

In an attempt to preserve Japanese traditions, the Japanese government has instituted a *Living Treasures* program, which grants official recognition and support to various cultural areas such as theater, music, dance, sculpture, carpentry, weaving, folk tradition, and arts and crafts. Ironically, Japan has not granted the same official recognition to its traditional methods of food-processing and production. This is in spite of the fact that increasingly large numbers of people throughout the world are appreciating the important health benefits of traditionally processed Japanese food products.

The Japanese traditional arts of producing miso, soy sauce, tofu, natto, amazake, rice vinegar, sake, mirin, condiments, and pickles, as well as their cooking and preparation methods are unique among the culinary practices of the world. These food-processing traditions require complete dedication, hard labor, thorough knowledge, and unwavering attention to the quality and combinations of ingredients, atmospheric conditions, and precise application methods.

These foods should be considered works of art; they are the source of health, happiness, and peace; they make up the fabric from which life itself is woven. Through these foods, all humanity will recover health, longevity, peace, and social stability. The humble, dedicated workers who have taken on the challenge of preserving these traditions (resisting the lure of commercialization and shallow business values) deserve both recognition and utmost respect. It is my sincere hope and recommendation that Japan's *Living Treasures* program officially recognizes and supports those who have dedicated their lives to the traditional art of food production and processing.

Mitoku Company, Ltd. shares my dream of a healthy, peaceful world. They, together with others of the same spirit, are preparing a foundation for the future of the world and its people. The history of Mitoku is a symbol of the history of the macrobiotic movement throughout the world. Hopefully, one day this history will be written to tell, in full, the story of how the macrobiotic movement was born, and the great role Mitoku played in bringing about the rebirth of humanity. I am very grateful to John and Jan Belleme for *Culinary Treasures of Japan*, their important contribution to this task.

Michio Kushi
Becket, Massachusetts

Preface

Years ago, the Japanese government took a bold and innovative step to help preserve the unique artistic heritage of Japan. Approximately seventy of Japan's finest artists and craftspeople were chosen to become living national treasures. Under a special *Living Treasures* program, older masters received government stipends to teach their skills to younger generations. This insured that the heart of Japanese culture would be kept alive.

Nothing is more basic to the existence of a culture than its food and cooking methods. Food makes the very blood needed to create the ideas that are eventually transformed into the artifacts of culture. Japan's island isolation has encouraged not only extraordinary arts and crafts, but also a unique way of making and preparing food. The skills and intuition required to make traditional Japanese foods, such as kuzu, shoyu, and snow-dried tofu, are just as important to the preservation of Japan's unique heritage as is the art of making pottery and fine rice paper.

Mitoku Company and others interested in distributing traditionally made Japanese foods recommend that the Japanese government include traditional food makers in the *Living Treasures* program. We feel the only difference between hand-made brown rice vinegar and hand-crafted lacquerware is in the materials that are used. Both hand-crafted arts and hand-made foods contain the spirit of the maker and the spirit of acient Japan.

Over the years, Mitoku Company, Ltd. has searched for the finest traditionally made Japanese foods for worldwide distribution. The map below shows the locations of the large companies and small shops where these high-quality products are processed or cultivated.

1. Johsen Shoyu
2. Mansan Tamari
3. Hatcho Miso
4. Onozaki Miso
5. Sakurai Noodles
6. Kojima Mochi
7. Nagata Teas
8. Ryujin Umeboshi
9. Kyushu Brown Rice Vinegar
10. Mikawa Mirin
11. Hiraide Sesame Oil
12. Akizuki Wild Kuzu
13. Snow-Dried Tofu
14. Uchida Brown Rice Malt
15. San-Riku Sun-Dried Wild Wakame
16. Boshu Sun-Dried Whole Wild Hijiki
17. Hidaka Sun-Dried Kombu
18. Ise Wild Arame
19. Sendai Select Nori
20. Snow-Dried Kanten Flakes
21. Snow-Dried Donko Shiitake

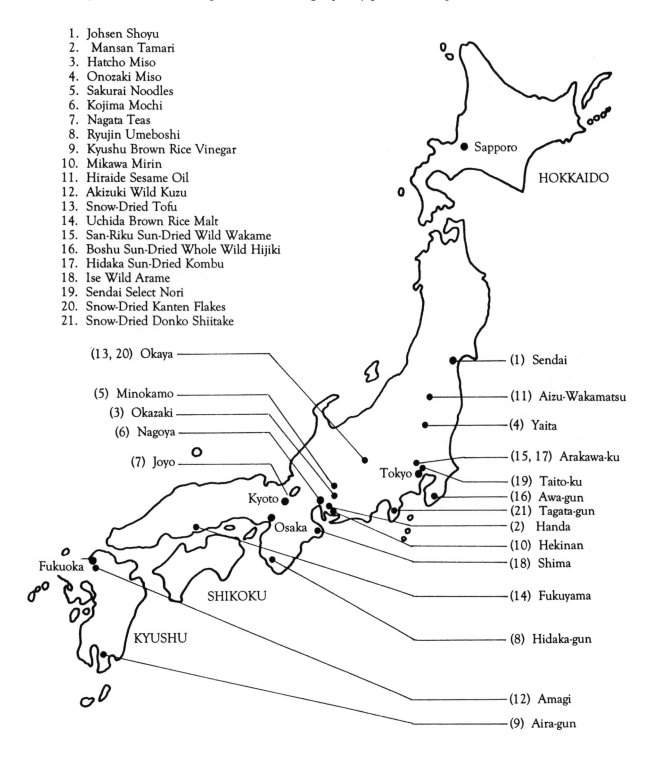

1

KUZU

The Wonder Root

Roots are the focal points of a plant's energy. This is why roots have always occupied a special place in man's diet, as well as in his medicine chest. Popular roots such as ginseng, dock, radish, beets, and carrots are prized for their concentrated food value and healing power. No wonder kuzu root (also spelled kudzu), one of the world's largest vegetable roots, is considered big medicine in Japan and China. Averaging 200 pounds, the kuzu root is an Oriental giant. The traditional medicine of choice for a host of digestive disorders, kuzu is also the world's premier cooking starch.

Kuzu also has a dark side. A sea of green tendrils and leaves that blankets seven million acres of the southeastern United States from May to October, kuzu smothers utility poles, trees, and barns. This prolific vine causes millions of dollars in damage each year. It's no wonder that kuzu has been jokingly referred to as "a vegetable form of cancer" and "the weed that ate Dixie."

Ironically, while irate farmers and utility companies have been killing kuzu by spraying and burning the plants, for years Asian people in the United States have been importing kuzu roots and root powder for medicinal and culinary use. In fact, one pound of the finest imported kuzu-root powder sells for about fifteen dollars in the United States.

THE SAGA OF KUZU IN AMERICA

Kuzu's schizophrenic existence in America began around the beginning of the 1900s, shortly after it was introduced from Japan. With purple wisteria-like flowers perfuming the summer air and cattle grazing on its large high-protein leaves, kuzu seemed like a perfect plant for southern farmers. Moreover, kuzu's large penetrating root system and nitrogen-fixing capability made it ideal for building soil and preventing soil erosion.

By the 1950s, however, many of kuzu's advocates had become disillusioned. Indeed, it was kuzu's incredible vitality that was causing the problem. Unchecked by its natural Asiatic enemies, kuzu enjoyed perfect growing conditions in the South and began to grow out of control. Under these conditions, according to Japanese foods scholar and author William Shurtleff (co-author of *The Book of Kudzu*), kuzu can grow one foot a day. One acre of neglected vines can cover thirteen-thousand acres in one hundred years!

In the 1960s, kuzu was partially redeemed because of America's growing interest in everything Japanese. Students of macrobiotics, Zen, and Oriental medicine began learning about kuzu's nutritional and medicinal value. It was even rumored that kuzu was the main food of the mysterious *sen-nin*, the Japanese mountain hermits who lived a life of simple austerity in order to find immortality through self-purification.

Kuzu soon became a respected food and medicine among macrobiotic and health-conscious consumers. Basic kuzu cream with umeboshi (see *Kuzu Power*, page 5) was found to be a very effective remedy for an acid stomach and for intestinal inflammation. Kuzu's mild taste, translucent sheen, and good jelling ability made it popular in puddings, sauces, stews, and glazes (see *Cooking With Kuzu*, page 7).

The final twist in the American kuzu saga took place recently in Alabama. A Japanese firm called Sakae Bio purchased 160 acres of land near Opelika, Alabama to grow kuzu. The firm plans to grow and harvest kuzu and then process it into powder for export to Japan. This is the first time kuzu will be cultivated commercially. (In Japan, only wild roots are harvested.)

KUZU IN NATIVE JAPAN

In its native land, kuzu has always enjoyed an excellent reputation. Asians seem to have no problem using kuzu as fast as it grows. Since ancient times, the leaves and roots have been used for food. The strong fibrous stems have been used as thread to weave fabrics and baskets. But it is kuzu cuisine that has become a fine art in Japan. The purest white kuzu-root powder is sought after by high-quality confection manufacturers and chefs of fine expensive restaurants.

According to Robbie Swinnerton, a British food columnist who has studied food manufacturing in Japan for over a decade, the techniques for processing kuzu were probably brought to Japan from China. By the twelfth century, farmers around the city of Kyoto had discovered how to process kuzu root in such a way that the starch was separated from its tough inedible fibers. About that time, kuzu powder began to be used in food preparation around the cities of Kyoto and Nara.

The first place kuzu starch was prepared for commercial purposes was established in the Yamato province in the early 1600s at the foot of Mount Yoshino. However, as civilization gradually pushed out into the mountainside, land became too valuable to grow wild kuzu. Kuzu-root-powder manufacturers were forced to move to Japan's more remote southern island of Kyushu. Today, almost all the kuzu-root powder used in Japan comes from a few large producers in Kyushu.

MAKING AKIZUKI KUZU

Today, Japan's largest kuzu-root-powder maker is the Hirohachido Company, located at the edge of Kagoshima Bay in southern Kyushu. Hirohachido makes three hundred tons of kuzu-root powder annually. This represents about two-thirds of Japan's total production. Fifth-generation president Kazuhiro Taguchi is head of the family-run business, which was founded in 1875. The original shop was in Akizuki, a small town in northern Kyushu. In 1953, the march of civilization pushed the Taguchi family further south to their present location.

Akizuki's climate and water are ideal for processing kuzu-root powder. What's more, according to Taguchi, the modern equipment used at their new factory in southern Kyushu subtly changed the quality of the kuzu-root powder. Determined to make the finest kuzu-root powder in all of Japan, Taguchi's father left a small group of workers at the Akizuki shop to continue the labor-intense, traditional hand process. The handmade kuzu powder made by Hirohachido Company at Akizuki is appropriately called Akizuki Kuzu. It is sold in natural foods stores around the world.

Kuzu Power

Kuzu (Pueraria lobata) *root's soothing medicinal effects have been known in Japan and China for over 1,000 years. The starch that makes kuzu-root powder an outstanding jelling and thickening agent in cooking is partly responsible for its strong medicinal action. Some of kuzu's complex starch molecules enter the intestines and relieve the discomfort caused by overacidity, bacterial infection, and—in the case of diarrhea—excess water. In many cases of abdominal aching and intestinal irritation, a bowl of kuzu gruel or pudding brings immediate relief.*

According to Dr. Subhuti Dharmananda, author and director of Institute for Traditional and Preventive Health Care in Portland, Oregon, kuzu has the same effect on the bowels as the herb slippery elm bark. The pectins in slippery elm, which have a chemical structure similar to kuzu's starch, cause similar jelling functions in food preparation. Like kuzu, slippery elm has been used for gastrointestinal irritation and diarrhea.

Although it is kuzu starch that is traditionally recommended for digestive problems, scientists have discovered that it is kuzu's particularly high flavonoid content that is responsible for its strong medicinal effect on the circulatory system. Flavonoids, and a related group of compounds known as bioflavonoids, occur naturally in plants and help regulate plant metabolism. However, they also have an influence on human physiology by dilating blood vessels that are constricted as a result of tension and stress.

The medicinal effects of kuzu's flavonoids were proven during research in Beijing, China. When given to human subjects, kuzu-root powder or its extracted flavonoids reduced high blood pressure; relieved chronic migraine headaches; and eased aches in the shoulders, neck, and head. Kuzu flavonoids have successfully treated sudden deafness, which can be caused by restricted circulation. In addition to relaxing blood vessels, flavonoids have been shown to lower cholesterol levels and reduce the risk of the formation of blood clots.

Medicinally, kuzu-root powder is used in two different basic ways: to make creamy beverages such as Kuzu Cream (recipe on page 8), and in combination with other herbs to make kuzu-root tea (known as kakkon tea in Japan). In Japan, kuzu-root tea is commonly used to treat allergies, especially hay fever, bronchial asthma, and skin rashes.

In the Far East, kuzu cream is used as a source of nutrition for the weak and elderly when solid food must be avoided. Recently, it was discovered that for those who are allergic to rice or wheat, a thick kuzu cream can be an alternative source of carbohydrates.

When made with the addition of ginger juice and minced umeboshi (salt-pickled plum), kuzu cream is especially potent. The ginger aids digestion and circulation, while the citric acid in the salt plum neutralizes lactic acid and eliminates it from the body. Lactic acid build-up in the body is thought to be related to numerous circulatory problems such as hardening of the arteries.

In his book Healing Ourselves, Macrobiotic teacher Naboru Muramoto recommends kuzu cream for colds, weak intestines, general body pains, stomach cramps, and diarrhea. Kuzu cream is also recommended for neutralizing stomach acidity and for relaxing tight muscles.

Since kuzu cream requires cooking, kuzu-root tea may be more convenient. Kuzu-root tea is found in herbal shops and some natural foods stores. Besides kuzu-root powder, this tea contains several other medicinal herbs such as ginger, licorice, cinnamon, and a wild grass from Mongolia called mao. Muramoto recommends kuzu-root tea for chronic headaches, stiff shoulders, colitis, upset stomach, breastfeeding difficulties, sinus troubles, tonsillitis, respiratory ailments, and hangovers.

It is obvious that, at least in the Far East, kuzu is considered a good general tonic. But you do not have to wait until you are sick to benefit from kuzu. Kuzu cream makes an excellent breakfast food, especially with a little added rice syrup. It's a great preventive medicine.

The 120-day process of making Akizuki Kuzu begins in December, when the kuzu plant has focused its energy back down underground and its roots are swollen with starch. The backbreaking work of hand digging roots in the mountains and backpacking them to the nearest road continues until the roots begin sending out their first shoots in the spring. In a good year, the roots will have about 13 percent extractable starch. If, however, there has been too much rain, too little sun, or if the previous autumn's typhoon has damaged the plant's leaves, the roots will produce less starch. When the starch level falls below 10 percent, it is not profitable for the Taguchis to process the roots.

The method of separating the starch from the fibrous kuzu root requires that the root be cleaned, cut, mashed, then washed repeatedly in cold water. After this initial stage, the crude gray kuzu paste is transported by truck from the large Hirohachido factory in southern Kyushu to the old shop at Akizuki.

At Akizuki, the crude paste is washed and filtered through silk screens many times to remove plant fibers and bitter tannins. After settling, the kuzu paste is redissolved in cold water and filtered again. The washing, filtering, and settling process continues until a pure white, clay-like starch is formed.

The starch is cut into 6-inch-thick blocks and placed in paper-lined boxes to dry for about sixty days. The drying process is critical. Kuzu cannot be dried in direct sunshine or heated ovens, as this will affect the purity of its color and impair its jelling qualities. Oven drying makes the kuzu too brittle and hard to dissolve in water. Proper drying takes place in a long wooden shed with large windows that are opened to circulate the air. Every few days, the boxes of kuzu are moved around to make sure each block dries evenly.

If the water used during the filtering process is not cold and pure, the kuzu will begin to ferment during drying. Too much humidity will cause bacterial fermentation and totally destroy the drying kuzu. When properly dried, each block of kuzu should contain about 16 percent moisture. Once dried, Akizuki Kuzu is carefully dusted with a soft hairbrush, crumbled, and packaged.

At Akizuki, fifteen workers produce only five or six tons of kuzu-root powder each season. At the large Hirohachido factory, forty-five workers make fifty times that amount.

According to Kazuhiro Taguchi, "Akizuki is blessed with an abundance of pure water and a perfect cold, dry winter, ideal for processing kuzu. The result," says Taguchi, "is kuzu that is unmatched in purity, dissolves quickly, has superior jelling ability, and gives foods a beautiful satin sheen." When pressed further, Taguchi claims that the molecular structure of handmade kuzu-root powder differs from the automated factory product. These subtle differences enhance kuzu-root powder's medicinal properties.

However, making kuzu in an automated factory is still a three-month-long, expensive process. The roots must still be dug by hand and then washed, filtered, and dried to extract the starch. In comparison, starch from sweet potatoes can be extracted in just three or four days with twice the yield as kuzu.

Because of kuzu's high price, many people use potato starch as a substitute. Some kuzu manufacturers mix potato starch with the kuzu powder. Shoppers must read labels carefully to be sure they are buying 100 percent kuzu powder. Kuzu sold in American Oriental foods stores is sometimes an inferior mix of potato and kuzu starch. However, kuzu-root powder sold in natural foods stores is usually high quality. Akizuki Kuzu is distributed under the Mitoku Macrobiotic label in the United States. Hirohachido Company's kuzu is available in North America under the Emperor's Kitchen, Erewhon, Kaiseki Select, and Tree of Life labels.

COOKING WITH KUZU

Kuzu is unsurpassed as a thickening agent. It produces sparkling, translucent sauces; adds a shiny gloss to soups; and provides a smooth texture for sauces and gravies with no starchy or interfering taste. Try using kuzu as a thickener in sauces and gravies, and for added body in soups and noodle broths. Vegetables and fish that have been dusted with kuzu powder and then deep-fried have a light, crisp coating. Since kuzu helps balance the acidity of sweets, it is ideal in desserts such as kantens and puddings, and it is the perfect ingredient in icings, shortcake toppings, and pie fillings.

Store kuzu in a sealed jar. When you buy kuzu, the powder will be in small chunks. Always crush the chunks with the back of a spoon before measuring. Use approximately 1 $\frac{1}{2}$ tablespoons of kuzu per cup of liquid for sauces and gravies and 2 tablespoons per cup for jelling liquids. For most preparations, completely dissolve the measured amount of kuzu in a little cold water, then add it to the other ingredients near the end of cooking time. Gently bring the mixture to a simmer, stirring constantly while the kuzu thickens and becomes translucent.

Kuzu should not be confused with arrowroot, potato starch, and corn starch. Corn starch, in particular, is not recommended because it is highly processed and treated with chemical bleaches and toxic extracting agents. Potato starch is also mass-produced, and chemicals are used to accelerate the extraction process. While arrowroot is made by a simple, natural process, kuzu is far superior in jelling strength, taste, texture, and healing qualities.

KUZU RECIPES

Kuzu Cream

This rejuvenating tonic is most effective when taken about one hour before meals (preferably in the morning when the stomach is empty). The recipe below makes a thick cream. If a thinner, beverage-like cream is desired, reduce amount of kuzu to 1 heaping teaspoon. Refer to Kuzu Power (beginning on page 4) for more information on the benefits of kuzu cream.

1 cup cold water
1 ½ tablespoons crushed kuzu
1 umeboshi plum, pitted and minced,
or 1 teaspoon umeboshi paste
¼–½ teaspoon fresh ginger juice
½–1 teaspoon shoyu (optional)

Yield: 1 cup

1. In a small enamel or nonmetallic saucepan, thoroughly dissolve kuzu in water.

2. Add umeboshi and bring to a simmer over medium heat, stirring frequently. As soon as mixture begins to bubble around the edges, stir constantly until kuzu thickens and becomes translucent. Gently simmer 1–2 minutes, then remove from heat.

3. Add ginger and shoyu (if desired) to taste.

Creamy Celery-Leek Soup

A creamy, warming fall and winter favorite.

1 large or 2 small leeks
8 celery stalks, finely chopped (including leaves)
1–2 teaspoons light sesame or canola oil
6 cups water or vegetable stock
6-inch piece kombu
1 teaspoon sea salt
Pinch white pepper (optional)
$\frac{1}{2}$ bay leaf
3 tablespoons crushed kuzu
2 level tablespoons mellow white miso
Chopped parsley for garnish

Serves: 6

1. Slit leeks lengthwise to center, remove any dirt between layers, and thinly slice.

2. Heat oil in a skillet, and sauté leeks over medium heat 2 minutes. Add celery and pinch of sea salt, and sauté a few minutes more.

3. In a medium-sized pan, place water or vegetable stock and kombu. Bring to a simmer, uncovered, over medium heat. As soon as liquid begins to simmer, remove kombu and reserve for another use.

4. To the stock, add salt, pepper, bay leaf, and sautéed vegetables. Simmer until celery is tender (15 to 20 minutes).

5. Purée soup in blender. Strain to remove tough fibers. Return soup to pan.

6. Thoroughly dissolve kuzu in an equal amount of cold water and add to soup while stirring. Bring soup back to a simmer while stirring constantly. Simmer 1–2 minutes more. Remove from heat.

7. Dissolve miso in 1 or 2 tablespoons water and add to soup. Serve hot with garnish of chopped parsley.

Sesame "Tofu"

This rich, creamy side dish is a favorite recipe of Kazuhiro Taguchi, president of Hirohachido Kuzu Company. The appearance and texture of the finished dish closely resembles silken tofu.

1 cup crushed kuzu

6 cups water

1 cup tahini

Shoyu, to taste

Peeled and finely grated ginger to garnish

Serves: 8–10

1. Thoroughly dissolve kuzu and water in medium-sized pan. Mix in tahini.

2. Bring to a simmer over medium heat. As soon as mixture begins to bubble, stir briskly and vigorously to prevent lumping and to assure a smooth texture. Continue stirring vigorously approximately 5 minutes.

3. Pour into a casserole or similar container and chill until firm.

4. Slice into small sections. Sprinkle shoyu (to taste) over individual servings. Top with a dab of grated ginger, and serve.

5. Refrigerate leftovers.

Clear Gravy

Unlike most sauces or gravies, this simple recipe contains little oil and no flour, yet it has a full, delicate flavor and pleasing texture. Serve over grains, vegetables, and noodles.

2 cups Dashi *(page 105)*
1 teaspoon sesame oil
1 small onion, minced
$\frac{1}{2}$ small bay leaf
$\frac{1}{4}$ teaspoon sea salt
1 tablespoon shoyu or tamari
$\frac{1}{2}$ tablespoon mirin (optional)
3 tablespoons crushed kuzu

Yield: 2 cups

1. Prepare stock.

2. Heat oil in a medium-sized skillet or small saucepan. Add onion and sauté 2–3 minutes.

3. Add stock, bay leaf, and salt. Gently simmer together 10–15 minutes.

4. Add mirin and shoyu or tamari, and cook 1 minute. Remove from heat.

5. Thoroughly dissolve kuzu in 3 tablespoons cold water and slowly add to sauce while stirring briskly. Return pan to heat and bring to a simmer, stirring constantly. Simmer 1–2 minutes.

6. Keep gravy hot (not boiling) until serving.

Vanilla Pudding

Vanilla pudding and the flavor variations suggested are delicious when eaten plain or when topped with fresh fruit or Fruit Sauce (recipe on page 13). These puddings also make great fillings for pies, parfaits, trifles, cream puffs, and shortcake. Almond milk is preferred over soymilk when making puddings. Almond milk has a pure white color, a fuller, richer flavor, and is more digestible.

2 cups Almond Milk (recipe on page 82) or plain soymilk
$\frac{1}{2}$ cup rice malt
$\frac{1}{8}$ teaspoon sea salt
2 level tablespoons kanten flakes (agar-agar)
$1\frac{1}{2}$ tablespoons crushed kuzu
1 teaspoon vanilla extract

Yield: 4 servings

1. Combine $1\frac{3}{4}$ cups almond milk or soymilk, rice malt, and salt in a small saucepan. Sprinkle in kanten flakes and bring to a simmer over medium heat. Simmer 1 minute while stirring.

2. Thoroughly dissolve kuzu in remaining $\frac{1}{4}$ cup milk and add to saucepan while stirring briskly. Return to a simmer and cook 1–2 minutes. Remove from heat.

3. Mix in vanilla and divide among four small dessert cups. Chill, uncovered, until firm (about 2 hours).

VARIATIONS

*   *Lemon Pudding.* Add $1\frac{1}{2}$ tablespoons lemon juice and $1\frac{1}{2}$ teaspoons lightly grated lemon zest along with the vanilla.

*   *Berry Pudding.* Follow directions for *Vanilla Pudding* except blend $1\frac{1}{2}$ cups fresh raspberries or strawberries with the almond or soymilk before heating, and reduce amount of vanilla to $\frac{1}{2}$ teaspoon.

Fruit Sauce

This light fruit dessert is delicious when eaten as is. It can also be used to dress up other simple desserts. It makes a great topping for vanilla or lemon pudding, pies or tarts with a vanilla-pudding base, shortcake, vanilla cake, pancakes, and waffles. This fruit sauce is a scrumptious filling for crepes.

1 cup apple juice
⅓–½ cup rice malt
(use smaller amount with sweet fruits, larger amount with tart ones)
Pinch sea salt
2 ½ cups sliced or whole fresh fruit
(strawberries, blueberries, raspberries, nectarines, pitted cherries, etc.)*
2 tablespoons crushed kuzu or 3 tablespoons arrowroot

Yield: Approximately 3 cups

1. Combine juice, rice malt, and salt in a saucepan. Add fruit (if appropriate) and bring to a simmer, uncovered, over medium heat. Remove from heat.

2. Thoroughly dissolve kuzu or arrowroot in 2 tablespoons cool water and add to fruit mixture while stirring briskly. Place over medium-low heat and stir constantly until mixture returns to a simmer and thickens.

3. If using fruit that does not require cooking, place fruit in a ceramic or glass bowl and pour the hot liquid over it. Mix gently and cool in refrigerator. If fruit is already mixed in, transfer contents of the pot to a bowl and cool. The sauce will thicken as it cools.

4. Refrigerated in a covered container, this fruit sauce will keep for several days.

---

*Cut larger fruits into small bite-sized pieces. Delicate, tender fruits such as strawberries and raspberries should not be cooked. Ripe nectarines do not need cooking, but firmer fruits such as blueberries, cherries, and apples should be simmered with the juice.

2

MIRIN

Sweet Rice Wine

Neighbors of Toshio Sumiya jokingly attribute his constant smile to the intoxicating vapors of the fermenting sweet rice wine that he is always inhaling. However, head brewmaster Sumiya protests that it is not just the heady aroma of the workplace that lifts his spirits, but the pride he feels in his family business. Sumiya Bunjiro Shoten, located in the small coastal town of Hekinan in central Japan, is one of the few authentic sweet rice wine producers in the entire country.

Once a thriving industry with over 200 companies, the processing of mirin—authentic sweet rice wine—did not survive the rice shortages of World War II or the post-war 76 percent liquor tax. As reported in the *Asahi Shimbun*, Japan's leading daily newspaper, by 1959, the Sumiya family business was the only company in Japan using the traditional methods of mirin brewing. Sumiya Bunjiro Shoten was sole keeper of the flame until recently, when a handful of companies began the production of authentic mirin.

In the early 1970s, the Sumiya family's perseverance and dedication to traditional standards paid off. Its mirin received five consecutive gold medals from the Alcoholic Seasonings Association. In 1975, the mirin produced by the Sumiya family became the only mirin ever to receive the coveted Diamond Award for excellence. Some five years later, Toshio Sumiya's international reputation was launched when Chris Dawson of Mitoku Company, Ltd. initiated the exportation of Sumiya Bunjiro Shoten mirin to five continents. Today, many major natural foods distributors carry Sumiya's mirin under one of its three United States labels—Mikawa, Mitoku Macrobiotic, and Emperor's Kitchen.

If you have not discovered authentic mirin, you are in for a treat. An exquisite, versatile seasoning, it has the unique ability to coax and accentuate the flavors from bland or light-tasting foods. Its mild sweetness balances many dishes and tones down others, such as seafoods. Mirin adds texture and an appetizing luster to foods that are glazed. With a little experience, you can use mirin in a variety of ways to enhance both Oriental and Western styles of cooking. Japan's traditional sweetener (before white sugar took over), mirin enhances the flavors of sweet as well as savory sauces, vinaigrettes, noodle broths, simmered vegetable and fish dishes, sautées and stir-fries, fried noodles, sushi rice, marinades, and dips for tempura and sushi. Cooking with authentic mirin is discussed in detail later in this chapter, but first, let's look at the deep-rooted history and traditional production of this uniquely Japanese food.

A TRADITIONAL ART

Mirin had its birth more than 500 years ago as a thick sweet drink. According to ancient Japanese texts, around the twelfth century, the Japanese began mixing cooked sweet glutinous rice with sake (rice wine) to enjoy as a festive drink. However, due to its high yeast and natural sugar content, this mirin-like beverage spoiled easily. In an effort to prolong shelf life, brewers in the warm southern islands began distilling this sweet rice-wine drink in the sixteenth century. The clear alcoholic concentrate that resulted, called *shochu* (literally, "fiery spirits") was about 80 proof and tasted somewhat like vodka. Shochu did not spoil in warm climates. Over the next few centuries, breweries in Japan's central region experimented by adding natural enzymes and sweet glutinous rice to the shochu. The mixture underwent long aging and purification, after which the thick sweet liqueur was bottled, becoming one of Japan's most exclusive and expensive alcoholic beverages. (Although mirin's 12–14 percent alcohol content is similar to that of wine, it is more closely related to liqueur or brandy because it is distilled.) Later, as its seasoning virtues were discovered, mirin became a dominant flavor in the traditional art of *kaiseki*, Japan's highest form of cooking.

MIRIN PRODUCTION: A WAY OF LIFE

In 1910, when Sumiya's grandfather started the family shop, the production of mirin was a complex, exacting process requiring years of experience to master. After serving a long apprenticeship, Sumiya's grandfather chose the perfect location to begin his own business, an area in central Japan known as Mikawa, where three great rivers flow into the Bay of Ise. Now part of the Aichi prefecture, this region is known for its mild climate, high-quality rice, and excellent water. As a result of these ideal conditions, Sumiya's grandfather was able to produce a mirin that was thick and rich beyond everyone's expectations. It was named Mikawa Mirin, literally "three-river mirin," in honor of its birthplace.

The labor-intense fermentation methods, still used by the Sumiya family, are steeped in the history and culture of pre-industrial Japan. More than a process, the family's work represents a way of life that, like Mikawa Mirin, is rare in the modern world.

At Sumiya Bunjiro Shoten, the year-long cycle begins in the fall with the making of *koji*, the 1,000-year-old ubiquitous catalyst that starts the fermentation of many important foods such as sake, rice vinegar, miso, shoyu, and tamari. The making of koji begins with one thousand pounds of locally grown rice that is polished to remove the oily outer bran (preventing an off-taste) and then soaked in spring water overnight. The following morning, the rice is steamed and then cooled until it is warm to the touch. Next, the Sumiya brothers sprinkle *Aspergillus* mold spores over the rice, mixing them in carefully so that each rice grain comes in contact with a microscopic spore. Finally, the warm inoculated rice is hurriedly carried to a uniquely constructed room called the *muro*. This traditional koji incubation room has three-foot-thick cedar-lined walls that are insulated with rice hulls.

Through the night, in the warm, humid condition of the muro, the mold spores germinate and send enzyme-laden filaments into the individual grains of rice. These filaments digest complex carbohydrates, transforming them into sweet sugars. By morning, the 1,000-pound mound of rice is fused together into a dense, damp mass. Using their hands and wooden shovels, the Sumiyas work through the morning breaking up the huge mound of rice into individual grains. They work in temperatures over 100°F with 100 percent humidity. While visitors cannot stand the stifling air of the muro for more than a few minutes, the Sumiyas, after decades of acclimatization, work at a relaxed pace, stopping briefly to gossip or to wipe the perspiration from their faces. After lunch, the rice is placed in dozens of wooden trays and left to ferment for a second night.

Through the night, as he has done since childhood, Toshio Sumiya visits the muro often to check the developing koji and to regulate the muro temperature by opening or closing the windows, which are located in the ceiling. After decades of making koji, the fifty-year-old Sumiya notes, "It's a world of mystery, which is better left to intuition than to modern technology." Early the next morning, he enters the warm, misty muro to taste the fluffy-white, glistening koji. With a confident nod, he signals to his brothers that the next phase of mirin making is ready to begin.

Although most mirin manufacturers, past and present, buy inexpensive shochu that has been distilled from molasses, the Sumiya family prepares its own from hand-made koji, premium rice, and spring water. These ingredients are mixed together and stirred each day for about a month. The resulting alcoholic mash, called *sake moromi*, is placed into cotton sacks, pressed, filtered, and distilled into clear rice shochu. This completes the first phase of authentic mirin processing.

. Next, 2,000 pounds of sweet glutinous rice are soaked and steamed. Stripped to the waist, Sumiya's youngest brother mounts a platform beside the rice steamer. Here he begins the backbreaking, hours-long task of shoveling the cooked sweet rice onto a cooling table. Before the day is over, he will repeat this process two more times, shoveling a total of three tons of rice. The cooked sweet rice is then added to the shochu together with more koji. This second mash, called *mirin moromi*, is placed in 1,000-gallon enamel vats that are insulated with rice-straw mats. With the exception of an occasional stirring, the mirin moromi is left to ferment for about three months. Gradually, the koji enzymes break down the complex carbohydrates and protein of the glutinous rice into sweet simple sugars and amino acids that blend with the shochu to form a delicious alcoholic rice pudding that, unfortunately, only traditional mirin manufacturers ever get to sample.

Standing over the huge vats, Sumiya sniffs the sweet rising vapors to judge the progress of the developing mash. A quick taste confirms what his nose has already discovered: It's time to pump the mash into cotton sacks and press out its sweet essence. (The remaining flavorful pressed moromi is used to make delicious mirin pickles.) Finally, this sweet essence (immature mirin) is returned to the enamel vats and left to age for about 200 days. During the hot days of the long Aichi summer, the subtle color and flavor of the mirin develops further. In the fall, Sumiya and his brothers eagerly sample their 70,000-gallon golden harvest and confirm that grandfather's recipe—unchanged after almost eighty years—yields mirin that is as delicious as ever. The mature mirin is then filtered through cotton and bottled, unpasteurized, for shipment to customers around the world.

Although there are now ninety mirin producers in Japan, only a few use the simple ingredients—sweet rice, koji, and shochu—and the traditional process just described. Some manufacturers buy inexpensive molasses shochu and use koji made by automated machines, then they add sweet rice or corn starch to make a quicker, less expensive mirin, which is rarely aged more than a few months. Denaturing agents such as salt are usually added to this inferior mirin so that liquor tax laws can be avoided. When asked how shoppers can tell if they are buying authentic mirin, Sumiya quickly replies, "It's the one you can drink." As we have seen, mirin had its beginning as a prized rice liqueur. However, the high-tech, syrupy, synthetic blend of glucose, corn syrup, ethyl alcohol, amino acids, and salt that sells for mirin today in the United States and Japan cannot be enjoyed as a beverage. It can serve only as a sugar substitute in some types of cooking.

So, if you want to toast the New Year with *O-toso* (see recipe on page 21) or add richness, balance, and luster to your cooking—rather than merely a sweet taste—read labels carefully. Authentic mirin contains rice, sweet rice, and water, and it has no additives or preservatives—surprisingly simple ingredients for such a complex, delicious, and versatile food.

COOKING WITH MIRIN

Mirin complements and balances the flavor of natural soy sauce in dishes. Although mirin, along with natural soy sauce (shoyu and tamari) and dashi (kombu stock), are known as the three essential tastes of old Japan, mirin was the missing ingredient in early American attempts at cooking with Japanese foods. Americans were quick to adapt salty Japanese seasonings such as miso, soy sauce, and umeboshi (salt-pickled plums), but the sweet taste and alcohol content of mirin was at first viewed with suspicion by natural foods shoppers. Consequently, prepared foods often lacked the balance and subtle sweetness of traditional Japanese cooking. However, as cooks began to realize that the simple ingredients comprising authentic mirin could be naturally transformed into an outstanding liquid seasoning, mirin grew in popularity.

Cooking Methods

Following are suggested tips for using mirin in both Oriental and Western cooking styles. Popular cooking methods as well as suggested uses for mirin are presented.

- **Making Nikiri Mirin.** Nikiri mirin is the name given to mirin after the alcohol has been burned off. Some Japanese cooks ignite warmed mirin before adding it to a dish in order to burn off the alcohol content. This step is not necessary when mirin is cooked into foods, since cooking quickly evaporates the alcohol.

If the aroma and flavor of the alcohol are undesirable when mirin is added to uncooked dishes, such as dips and sushi rice, simply heat the mirin just to the boiling point, then allow it to cool before adding it to the dish.

- **Sautéeing and Stir-Frying.** Mirin adds depth of flavor to sautéed and stir-fried vegetable, fish, and noodle dishes. Its high natural sugar content allows it to burn easily, so it is often incorporated into a dish toward the end of cooking. This helps enhance and round out the flavors while contributing to the richness of the dish.

- **Simmering.** Mirin is used to flavor many simmered and poached dishes including fish, shiitake mushrooms, reconstituted dried tofu, and deep-fried tofu. When simmering foods, use 1 tablespoon of mirin and $1-1\frac{1}{2}$ tablespoons of shoyu per cup of water or stock.

Suggested Uses

- **In Desserts.** Mirin is a delicious addition to such desserts as poached pears, fruit cakes, tea cakes, and glazes.

- **In Dips.** Dips for tempura and other deep-fried foods, such as mochi, almost always include mirin.

- **As a Liqueur.** Here is where the value of mirin made with traditional ingredients and unhurried, natural aging is most obvious. While other mirins and mirin-like seasonings are unable to be drunk, authentic mirin is delicious. Serve mirin chilled on ice or at room temperature, depending on the season. Enjoy it plain or with a little lime juice added. In Japan, mirin is sometimes served with ginger and hot water in the winter; it is also combined with certain herbs to make a delicious medicinal tonic.

- **In Marinades.** Sake or other wines act as tenderizers and are preferred for marinating fish and poultry. Mirin, on the other hand, makes food more firm and helps it maintain its texture and shape. Mirin marinade is best used as an enhancer of such tender foods as tofu; however, it is occasionally added in small amounts to fresh fish in order to help tone down the strong taste and aroma.

- **In Noodle Broths.** Mirin is the "secret" ingredient that lends a characteristic flavor to noodle broths and dips. Without mirin, these dishes tend to be flat.

- **In Sauces and Gravies.** A tablespoon of mirin can transform a ho-hum sauce into a rich, gourmet delight.

- **In Sushi.**   Before sugar became cheap and widely available, mirin was used along with salt and rice vinegar to season sushi rice. Mirin makes the rice soft yet firm and gives the grain a desirable glossy appearance.

O-toso

In traditional homes throughout Japan, the New Year is brought in with the ritual of drinking o-toso, a medicinal tonic. Made by infusing a combination of herbs in mirin—which is rich in natural sugars, amino acids, and digestive enzymes—o-toso is considered a nutritious health drink and is believed to protect one from sickness and misfortune.

Each member of the family has his or her own special cup, which is reserved for o-toso. Holding their cups, family members pray to spend the coming year free from sickness and to gain or preserve a youthful energy. O-toso is also served to guests on the first three days of the New Year as a symbolic fortification against the uncertainties of the future.

Although o-toso herbs, generally sold in tea bags, are not available in this country, you can create your own o-toso tonic using Mu-16 tea, which contains several of the medicinal herbs commonly used in o-toso blends. To prepare, infuse one Mu-16 tea bag in 10 ounces of mirin at room temperature for 7–8 hours, no longer. Carefully remove the tea bag. The o-toso is now ready for your New Year's toast: To your good health!

MIRIN RECIPES

Green Beans Amandine

Miso-mirin sauce transforms plain vegetables into something you will be proud to serve. Other vegetables such as sliced parsnips or thinly sliced cabbage can be substituted for the green beans.

2 teaspoons sesame or high-oleic safflower oil
$1/3$ cup slivered almonds
3 $1/2$ cups green beans, thinly sliced on the diagonal
Pinch sea salt
3 tablespoons mellow white miso
3 tablespoons mirin

Serves: 4

1. Heat oil in a medium-sized skillet over medium heat. Add almonds and sauté 2–3 minutes.

2. Add green beans and salt, and sauté 1–2 minutes more.

3. Add water to just cover bottom of the pan. Cover and steam until beans are just tender and still colorful.

4. Combine miso and mirin, and add mixture to vegetables. Toss and cook 1 minute more, adding more water if needed.

Marinated White Fish Fillets

This simple dish enhances the delicate flavor of fresh white fish. It takes little time to prepare and, when properly cooked, is absolutely delicious.

3 tablespoons mirin

1 tablespoon shoyu

3–4 thin slices ginger root, diagonally cut

1 pound white fish fillets
(flounder, sole, snapper, scrod, sea bass, orange roughy, etc.)

Cabbage leaves to steam fish on (or heat-proof plate)

1 tablespoon sesame oil,
or combination of 2 teaspoons light and 1 teaspoon toasted sesame oil

Dash chili oil (optional)

1 rounded teaspoon ginger, peeled and cut into thin strips

1 scallion, cut on the diagonal into thin 1 1/2-inch strips

Serves: 3

1. Combine mirin and shoyu in large shallow dish. Completely coat fillets with this mixture, tuck ginger slices under fillets, and let marinate for 20–30 minutes, turning once.

2. Arrange fish on heat-proof plate or steamer tray lined with cabbage leaves. Steam fish over rapidly boiling water until just white throughout and flaky (about 9 minutes for each inch of thickness).

3. If desired, transfer fillets to platter or individual serving dishes. (If using bamboo steamer lined with cabbage leaves, serve as is.)

4. In small skillet, heat sesame oil and chili oil (if using). Add ginger strips and scallions, and sauté 30 seconds. Immediately spoon heated mixture over fish.

5. Serve immediately.

Glazed Acorn Squash

This golden treat makes a perfect side dish for a holiday meal.

*1 small acorn squash, quartered, seeded, peeled,
and cut crosswise into $\frac{1}{3}$-inch-wide slices*
$\frac{1}{2}$ *cup water*
$\frac{1}{4}$ *cup mirin*
$\frac{1}{2}$ *cinnamon stick*
3–4 whole cloves
Pinch sea salt

Serves: 4

1. Combine all ingredients in medium saucepan and bring to a boil. Lower heat and gently simmer, covered, until squash is tender (15–20 minutes). With a slotted spoon, immediately transfer squash to a heated dish. Keep warm in a preheated 170°F oven.

2. Strain cooking liquid and return to pot. Cook liquid down, uncovered, to half the volume (about 3 tablespoons). Check frequently to avoid burning.

3. Pour glaze over squash and serve.

Teriyaki Tofu

Unexpected guests? This flavorful dish is quick and simple to prepare.

1 pound (1 large block) tofu
3 tablespoons mirin
2–2 ½ tablespoons shoyu or tamari (to taste)
2(3 teaspoons sesame oil (plain or toasted)
1 teaspoon peeled and finely grated ginger
2 tablespoons finely minced scallion

Serves: 5

1. Cut tofu crosswise into five equal slices. To remove excess moisture, wrap slices in a clean, dry kitchen towel and place on a wooden cutting board. Place a 2–3 pound weight on top and leave for 20–30 minutes.

2. Lay slices flat on a platter or baking pan.

3. Combine mirin and soy sauce, then pour mixture over tofu slices. Coat tofu on all sides and let marinate 15–20 minutes. Turn slices once or twice while marinating.

4. Heat oil in a large skillet (cast iron or other heavy-bottomed pan works best) over medium-low heat. Remove tofu from marinade and set marinade aside.

5. Drain excess liquid from tofu and fry on one side until lightly browned. (Browning will enhance tofu's flavor and appearance, but be careful not to burn.) Carefully turn slices and cook 2–3 minutes more.

6. With paper towel, blot any excess oil left in the skillet, then add marinade and cook another 30 seconds.

7. Place tofu slices on individual serving dishes. Top each slice with ½ teaspoon of remaining liquid from pan. If desired, sprinkle slices with a few drops of juice squeezed from the grated ginger.

8. Garnish with minced scallion and serve hot.

Cider-Poached Pears

This simple dessert provides a warm, sweet ending to fall or winter meals.

3 ripe but firm pears, halved and cored
Apple juice
Water
1 teaspoon cider-spice mixture
(or 1 cinnamon stick and several whole cloves)
Pinch sea salt
1 tablespoon mirin
1 tablespoon crushed kuzu
Walnuts or pecans for garnish (optional), chopped and toasted

Serves: 6

1. Arrange single layer of pear halves on bottom of a medium-sized saucepan.

2. Pour in mixture of 3 parts apple juice and 1 part water to almost cover pears. Add spices and salt. Simmer, covered, until pears are tender.

3. Remove pears with slotted spoon, drain, and place in small individual bowls.

4. Strain liquid, then return it to pan. Cook liquid down to 1 cup. Add mirin.

5. Thoroughly dissolve kuzu in 1 tablespoon cold water and add to cider while stirring briskly. Continue stirring over medium-low heat until kuzu thickens and becomes translucent. Simmer 1 minute more.

6. Immediately ladle sauce over pears. If desired, add a sprinkle of toasted nuts.

3

MISO

A Health Secret to Savor

Miso, a fermented soyfood, is one of the world's most delicious, versatile, and medicinal foods. This ancient Far Eastern staple recently began appearing on natural foods store shelves in the West but has already established itself as an essential ingredient in the new natural cuisine. Miso is used to enhance every course from hors d'oeuvres to desserts. It is used in basic macrobiotic dishes as well as fancy gourmet fare.

It is no wonder that miso quickly became popular among health-conscious Americans. A good source of essential amino acids and some vitamins and minerals, miso is also low in calories and fat. Centuries of Japanese folklore and recent scientific studies indicate that the daily use of miso may lower cholesterol, alkalinize the blood, cancel the effects of some carcinogens, counteract the effects of radiation exposure, and neutralize the effects of smoking and environmental pollution. Like yogurt, unpasteurized miso is abundant in lactic-acid bacteria and enzymes that aid in digestion and food assimilation (see *Miso Medicine*, page 36).

Miso Types

Traditionally, miso is made by combining koji (cultured grain or soybeans used as a starter in most Japanese fermented foods) with cooked soybeans, salt, and water. This mixture is then left to ferment. By varying the type of koji used (usually rice, barley, or soybean) and the proportions of ingredients in the recipe, traditional miso makers were able to create a wide range of misos, from light and sweet to dark and robust.

Although there are a few exceptions, misos can be divided into two groups based on color and taste. Sweet miso is usually light in color (beige or yellow) and high in carbohydrates. It is marketed as mellow miso, sweet miso, and sweet white miso. Because it is high in koji and low in soybeans and salt, sweet miso ferments in just two to eight weeks, depending on the exact recipe and the temperature used during the aging process. These misos developed and became popular around Kyoto and Japan's southern regions.

Miso with a higher salt content, lower koji content, and proportionately more soybeans is darker in color and saltier in taste than sweet miso. It must be fermented longer (at least one summer, but usually as long as two to three years) in very cold climates. This type of miso is marketed as red miso, brown rice miso, and barley miso. Soybean misos, such as mame and hatcho, are also dark and savory. Salty, long-aged misos are more popular in Japan's central and northern regions.

METHODS FOR MISO MAKING

Miso is such a unique and vital food that it is important to understand what factors influence its taste, medicinal qualities, and nutritional value. The two most important influences on all three of these qualities are manufacturing methods and the quality of ingredients used.

Basically there are two methods for making miso—commercial and traditional. The modern commercial process employs accelerated temperature-controlled fermentation in plastic or stainless steel holding tanks. The grains and salt used in the commercial method are often processed and have little nutritional value.

The slower traditional method employs natural aging in large wooden fermentation casks at the temperature of the environment. Traditional manufacturers, such as those presented in this chapter, use whole ingredients and natural sea salt.

Although commercial miso manufacturers claim their product is similar to the more expensive, traditionally made varieties, Mitoku Company's Chris Dawson disagrees. Dawson compares natural miso fermentation to raising children: "If you leave children inside year round with air conditioning and artificial heat, they will not develop the resistance, strength, health, and character of children that play outside in the extremes of winter and summer. Likewise, temperature-controlled miso lacks vitality, character, and complexity." More than just a method, making traditional miso is a way of life.

When choosing miso, look for traditionally made, unpasteurized miso, then let your personal needs, taste, and seasonal considerations be your guide.

RICE AND BARLEY MISOS

Hoping to learn the art of making natural miso, in the fall of 1980, we set out for Japan to find a miso master with a big heart and willingness to teach. With the help of Akiyoshi Kazama, president of Mitoku Company, we found such a man, Takamichi Onozaki. Onozaki makes several organic barley and brown rice misos for Mitoku. Our eight-month stay with the Onozaki family had a profound, positive influence on our lifestyle, health, and appreciation for traditional Japanese food and culture.

Our first few weeks in rural Japan were cultural vertigo. However, a combination of Mr. Onozaki's faith and patience, combined with our driving passion to learn his art got us through the early days with minimum embarrassment.

ONOZAKI FAMILY: TRADITIONAL MISO MAKERS

The Onozaki family makes traditional miso; traditional in the sense that their basic methods have been the same for generations. Although they recently purchased simple equipment to accommodate the ever-increasing demand for their miso, their methods of making koji and of miso fermentation have remained unchanged from that of their ancestors.

The labor involved is intense. The body is exposed to extremes of hot and cold. At first it seemed that we were beyond our limits of endurance. Taking inventory

The koji is placed in wooden boxes, which are stacked around the room.
By morning, the koji is mature.

of sore body parts became a morning ritual. The Onozaki lifestyle—living under natural conditions with little heat and strong food—soon provided us with the strength and stamina we needed.

Each six-and-a-half-day weekly miso-making cycle is almost exactly the same. First, the koji is made, then, later in the week, the soybeans are prepared. Finally, at the end of the week, the beans are mixed with koji, salt, and water to make miso.

The Onozakis' typical weekly cycle—omitting details—goes as follows: First 1,500 pounds of pearled barley or lightly milled rice are washed, soaked overnight, and then steamed the following morning. The hot grain is taken from the steamer and cooled until it is just warm to the touch. Next, *Aspergillus oryzae* spores (tane koji) are hand rubbed into the warm grain. The inoculated grain is then carried into a dark, thick-walled, dirt-floored koji room, and it is placed on a long crib in the middle of the room. After being covered with four or five blankets, the inoculated grain is left overnight for incubation.

By morning, the inoculated grain has begun early koji fermentation. By the time it is uncovered, it is a 1,500-pound mountain of grains, loosely held together by the growing *Aspergillus* mold. The next task is to separate each grain by handrubbing, mixing the cooler surface rice with the warmer bottom rice.

Usually four people, bending over the low table, sliding their open hands over the warm rice or barley, work in rhythm. They start at one end of the mound in the early morning and work their way down to the other end by the early afternoon. The process presents an amazing sight, a timeless ritual. Huddled around the low table, everyone works in silence. Hair is covered with scarves to keep sweat from entering the eyes. Steam rises from the lower levels of the koji. Occasionally the workers stop to comment on their progress or to wipe perspiration from their faces.

To our surprise, this job became a labor of love for us. We welcomed the ever-changing sweet smell of fermenting grain and the soothing feeling we experienced when we put our cold hands into the warm rice or barley on a frosty winter morning. Most of all, we derived much satisfaction from working with nature to produce a delicious living food.

After being mixed and separated, the koji is placed in small wooden boxes and stacked around the walls of the koji room in "bricklap stacks" to allow air circulation. Temperature and humidity—both very important to good koji growth—are regulated by the opening and closing of ceiling vents through the night. By the following morning, the koji is mature. A fine delicate web of glistening threads covers the surface of the rice in each box.

Later in the week, 1,500 pounds of hand-selected soybeans are washed, cooked, cooled, and crushed. Finally Takamichi-san's wife, guided by years of experience, directs the mixing of crushed beans, koji, salt, and water to make 120 pounds of miso. Each 120-pound batch is placed in four buckets and relayed to a person standing on a ladder atop a huge six-ton-capacity cedar vat. With a loud thud, the first few batches hit the bottom of the empty vat. In five or six days the seven-foot-tall vat is full.

The slow process of fermentation begins almost immediately. Some miso masters add 5 to 10 percent of their mature miso—called "seed miso"—as a catalyst to start fermentation. Takamichi-san does not; he relies on the bacteria already present in his 200-year-old vats to start the fermentation process. Through the long family history, these bacteria have been naturally selected; they are strong and well-adapted to miso fermentation.

The bacteria, aided by enzymes in the koji, start the long, natural fermentation of soybeans and rice. Proteins and oils are gradually digested into simple amino and fatty acids. As the miso darkens, a delicious, almost black liquid called tamari gathers in pools around the inside of the vat. The rapidly multiplying bacterial population, eager for a source of food to support their growing numbers, converts complex carbohydrates to maltose, glucose, ethyl alcohol, and organic acids, giving off a deep, rich aroma that fills the room.

Under the natural conditions of the open miso storage room, the fermentation rate adjusts to the changing seasons. Lying almost dormant in the winter, the bacteria are gradually awakened by the warmth of spring and are stimulated into a frenzy of activity by the hot summer sun. Takamichi-san likes his miso to have the benefit of at least two summers. The Onozakis make over 100 tons of traditional miso each year, a sizable production considering the simplicity of equipment and size of the labor force. (Using a modification of their basic methods, the Onozakis also make sweet miso, which matures in just thirty days.)

Each day after work, we would eat dinner, then talk or study for a few hours, take a scalding bath, and get out the futon. By 10:30 p.m. only the cats playing on the roof disturbed the tranquility of the darkened house. Like a mantra, the calming effects of our daily life gave us strength and peace of mind. It was a natural rhythm, a reflection of nature, like the slow rising and falling of breath during deep meditation.

AN ONGOING TRADITION

As fall turned to winter and the room temperature of the unheated house dropped to below 0°C, the kotatsu (heated table) became the focus of our night life. It was on such a night toward the end of our stay, while we huddled together on the living room floor, that Takamichi-san showed us his ancient family scroll. Beginning with the Onozaki family on the east coast of Japan around 1200 A.D., it recorded the birth, life, and death of each first-born son down to Takamichi-san's father, who had died just two years earlier. In ancient script, it told of the family's early farming existence, its gradual ascent to samurai lordship, and the continuous struggle to maintain its domain against overwhelming forces. When we asked detailed questions, Takamichi-san scanned the ancient paper, which was stretched out across the length of the living room floor.

A blank space, reserved for Takamichi-san, was at the far end of the scroll. Takamichi had no sons; he is the last Onozaki. This was, no doubt, on his mind. A month later, not long before we prepared to return to America with our new craft, he presented us with a beautiful black lacquer box, which had a picture of his kin's coat of arms on the lid. In this way Takamichi-san seemed to be telling us that we were a small, ongoing part of his family.

COOKING WITH RICE OR BARLEY MISO

The key to fine miso cooking is not to overpower dishes with a strong miso taste. The more subtle aspects of miso color and flavor should be integrated to create a gentle balance with other ingredients.

The light color, sweet taste, and creamy texture of sweet miso is suggestive of its application in American-style cooking: it is an excellent dairy substitute. For example, try a little sweet miso instead of milk in mashed potatoes or creamed soups. Try combining tofu with sweet miso and lemon or rice vinegar to make creamy dips and spreads. To realize the full potential of sweet miso, explore its uses in salad dressings and sauces. Mellow white miso and good-quality rice vinegar create a delicate tartness that is both refreshing and cooling. Sweet miso combined with sake or mirin make excellent sauces for baked, broiled, or stir-fried vegetables or fish. Think of sweet miso for festive occasions and light summer cooking. In southern climates, mellow barley miso is excellent for year-round cooking.

The readily digestible amino acids, fatty acids, and simple sugars; and the relatively low-salt content of sweet miso makes it ideal for the delicate constitutions of babies and young children. A very diluted mellow-miso broth is readily accepted by most children starting at age six months.

In contrast, dark, saltier miso is excellent for basic winter cooking in cold climates. Its hearty quality combines nicely with beans, gravies, baked dishes, and vegetable stews and soups. Try dark miso in thick soups with root vegetables such as burdock, carrots, and daikon. A lentil loaf made with red miso warms the body and supplies a large quantity of high-quality protein. Remember that dark miso is stronger in taste than sweet miso, so use it sparingly.

Any discussion of miso is incomplete without considering its use in miso soup. Miso soup and rice, accompanied by a side dish of pickles and a cup of tea, constitutes a meal by Japanese standards. In Japan, the dynamic flow of ingredients, texture, and color of miso soup reflects seasonal changes and geographic location. In the south, sweet barley miso, which gives miso soup a beautiful yellow to beige color, is preferred. In the north, hearty red miso is the popular choice. Often combined with carrots, burdock, and wakame, red miso produces soup with a very earthy color and flavor. Don't be afraid to experiment with the many possibilities of miso soup. However, since miso is the dominant taste here, unpasteurized miso is used. Miso should be added to soup near the end of its cooking time. Miso (in miso soup) may be briefly simmered, but not boiled. Boiling alters the fresh miso flavor and destroys beneficial enzymes and microorganisms. A thick purée, the miso should be dissolved in some of the soup stock before being added to the soup.

According to ancient Japanese mythology, miso was a gift from the gods. An integral part of a traditional Japanese diet, miso has evolved with other foods in that diet. Not only is miso closely associated with the Zen Buddhist grain-centered vegetarian diet, it is also linked with such foods as rice vinegar, sake, and mirin, which were often used with miso for the purpose of balance.

Miso Medicine

Miso's outstanding medicinal qualities have been confirmed by scientific research. Dr. Shinchiro Akizuki, director of Saint Francis Hospital in Nagasaki, devoted his career to researching the use of foods, such as miso, as preventive medicine. Although Dr. Akizuki spent years treating atomic-bomb victims just a few miles from ground zero, neither he nor his associates suffered from the usual effects of radiation. Dr. Akizuki hypothesized that he and his staff were protected from the deadly radiation because they drank miso soup every day.

In 1972, Akizuki's theory was confirmed when researchers discovered miso contains dipicolonic acid, an alkaloid that chelates heavy metals, such as radioactive strontium, and discharges them from the body.

In 1981, scientists at Japan's Cancer Research Center found that those who regularly ate miso soup suffered significantly less than the norm from some forms of cancer and heart disease. More recently, workers at Tohoku University in Hokkaido, Japan, isolated substances in miso that cancel out the effects of some carcinogens.

The most convincing evidence demonstrating the protection miso offers to those exposed to radiation was published in Japan in 1990. Professor Akihiro Ito, at Hiroshima University's Atomic Radioactivity Medical Lab, read reports of European countries importing truckloads of hatcho miso after the accident at the Chernobyl nuclear power plant. Professor Ito reasoned that if people were protected from radiation by miso, then rats that were fed miso and radiated should develop less cancer than radiated rats that were not fed miso. Professor Ito was not surprised to find that the liver-cancer rate for the rats that were not fed miso was 100 to 200 percent higher than that of miso-fed rats. Even more extraordinary is the fact that Ito used commercial miso powder, the lowest quality of miso! Many natural healers and traditional Oriental physicians consider long-aged misos, such as hatcho miso, the most medicinally potent.

RICE AND BARLEY MISO RECIPES

Almost-Instant Miso Soup

A quick soup to make, this recipe requires almost no cooking. Substitute other vegetables, if desired, and cook until tender.

4 cups Dashi *(page 105)* or other vegetable stock
$1/3$ pound fresh tofu, cut into $1/2$-inch cubes
2 cups watercress, chopped into $1^1/2$-inch lengths
3 level tablespoons red *(rice)* or barley miso
Slivered scallion for garnish

Serves: 4

1. Prepare stock.

2. Bring stock to a simmer, add tofu and watercress, and simmer one minute. Remove from heat.

3. Dissolve miso in some of the broth, then return to the pot.

4. Ladle hot soup into individual serving bowls and garnish with scallions.

Corn-Miso Soup

Miso soup with fresh corn is our summer favorite. Boiling the cobs makes a delicious stock. When using other vegetables, remember to start with a tasty shiitake or vegetable stock.

2–3 ears fresh corn

6 cups water

6-inch-strip kombu

1 onion, diced

$\frac{1}{8}$ teaspoon sea salt

1 carrot, sliced into thin rounds

2–3 tablespoons minced parsley

2 tablespoons red (rice) miso
mixed with 3 tablespoons mellow white miso

Serves: 4–5

1. Remove corn kernels from cobs. In a medium-sized pot, combine cobs with water and kombu. Bring to a simmer, uncovered, then remove kombu and reserve for another use.

2. Gently simmer cobs 10 minutes, then remove and discard.

3. Add onion and sea salt, and simmer 10 minutes.

4. Add carrot and corn kernels, and simmer 10 minutes more.

5. Add parsley during last minute of cooking. Remove pot from heat.

6. Dissolve miso mixture in some of the broth, then return to the pot.

7. Serve piping hot.

Pinto Bean Soup

Served with whole grain bread, this thick, tasty soup makes a satisfying cool-weather lunch. As part of a nutritious full-course meal, Pinto Bean Soup goes well with your favorite whole grain and a side of greens.

2 cups dry pinto beans

1 tablespoon olive oil

1 onion, diced

2 cloves garlic, minced

3 medium carrots,
cut in half lengthwise, then thinly sliced into half-moons

1 rib celery, sliced (chop leaves, if any, and set aside)

1 $\frac{1}{2}$ teaspoons sea salt

1 large bay leaf, broken into 3 pieces

$\frac{1}{2}$ teaspoon dried marjoram or oregano

$\frac{1}{2}$ teaspoon dried basil

2 level tablespoons red (rice) or barley miso

Serves: 6–8

1. Soak beans in 6 cups water for 8 hours, or bring beans to a boil 2–3 minutes, remove from heat, and soak 1–2 hours.

2. Drain beans and combine with 8 cups water in a large pot. Bring to a boil, then reduce heat and simmer until beans are tender (1 $\frac{1}{2}$–2 hours).

3. Heat oil in a medium-sized skillet and sauté onion and garlic until translucent.

4. Add carrots and celery, and sauté briefly. Add water to cover and simmer, uncovered, 10 minutes.

5. When beans are tender, add salt, vegetables, bay leaf, and herbs. Simmer 15 minutes more.

6. Dissolve miso in some of the broth, then return to the pot. Serve piping hot.

Azuki-Squash Bake

Mildly sweet and hearty, this recipe produces a satisfying entrée for fall or winter meals.

1 cup dry azuki beans

2 ½ cups water

½ bay leaf

Pinch dried rosemary (optional)

1 teaspoon sesame oil

1 large onion, diced

2 ½ cups bite-sized pieces winter squash (butternut, acorn, or buttercup)

Pinch sea salt

2 level tablespoons red (rice) or barley miso

Chopped parsley for garnish

Serves: 4–5

1. Soak beans 2–3 hours, then discard soaking water.

2. Place beans in a pressure cooker with fresh water to cover and bring to a boil, uncovered. Simmer 5 minutes, then drain beans and discard liquid (this removes azuki beans' slightly bitter taste).

3. Add 2 ½ cups fresh water and the herbs. Cover and bring to pressure, lower heat, and cook for 45–50 minutes. (If pot-boiling instead of pressure cooking, simmer for 2–2 ½ hours, adding more water as needed.)

4. While beans are cooking, heat oil in a medium-sized pan and sauté onion until translucent and limp.

5. Add squash and sea salt, and sauté briefly. Lower heat, cover, and cook until squash is somewhat soft but not completely tender. (Check frequently. If necessary, add only enough water to prevent scorching.) Uncover and set aside.

6. Preheat oven to 375°F.

7. In a casserole dish, combine cooked beans, vegetables, and miso that has been thinned in two tablespoons water. Cover and bake 30-40 minutes.

8. Garnish with parsley and serve.

Miso Soup With Fu

6 cups Dashi *(page 105)*
4 fresh or reconstituted (dried) shiitake mushrooms, thinly sliced
1 ½ cups kale or mustard greens, chopped and tightly packed
1 piece shonai fu,* broken into bite-sized pieces
3-4 tablespoons barley or red (rice) miso (to taste)

Serves: 4

1. Prepare stock.

2. Add shiitake and simmer 5 minutes.

3. Add kale and fu, and simmer 10 minutes more, or until the kale is tender.

4. Remove from heat. Dilute miso in some of the broth, then return to the pot. Allow to steep briefly before serving.

---

*Shonai fu comes in thin, flat sheets. Other types of fu include kuruma (donut-shaped) and zeni (small donut-shaped).

Miso Pickles

Crisp, lightly pickled vegetables can be a part of every meal. Miso pickles are nutritious and easy to digest. They are easily prepared and ready to eat in 1–3 days. Be creative! In addition to the variations below, try pickling other vegetables. Experiment! For a stronger flavor, pickle for a longer period of time but serve smaller amounts. Very strong-flavored pickles can be minced and sprinkled sparingly over rice or millet.

Red (rice) or barley miso,
or combination of equal parts red miso and mellow white miso
(amount will vary depending on size of pickling container)
Root vegetables (carrots, turnips, rutabagas, etc.), sliced

1. Place 1-inch layer of miso in bottom of a non-metal container.

2. Add vegetables and cover with more miso.

3. Cover container and let sit, unrefrigerated, 2–3 days.

4. Remove vegetables, rinse, and serve.

5. If desired, cut vegetables into matchsticks before serving.

VARIATIONS

• Submerge whole cabbage leaves in miso and cover. After 1 day, remove leaves, rinse, and cut in half lengthwise. Then cut the halves crosswise into thin shreds.

• For celery pickles, cut stalks into lengths appropriate for container. Submerge stalks in miso, cover, and leave for 2–3 days. Rinse, slice on the diagonal, and serve.

• Cut tofu into $\frac{3}{4}$-inch slices, press out excess water, and submerge in miso. This pickled tofu will be ready in half a day. Refrigerate leftovers.

HATCHO MISO

In central Japan's Aichi Province, in the town of Okazaki, there is a curious set of old tile-roof buildings on Hatcho (8th) Street. These buildings are the home of Hatcho Miso Company, makers, for five centuries, of one of Japan's true living treasures, the most revered miso in all Japan. Under the ancient rafters of the shop stand rows of huge 200-year-old cedar casks, held together with hoops of braided bamboo and topped with a mountain of stones that are so skillfully arranged that they never collapse, even during earthquakes. In each vat, under the pressure of three tons of river rocks, 12,000 pounds of hatcho (pronounced hot-cho) miso slowly and naturally ferments through the hot, humid summers and mild Aichi winters. After twenty-four to thirty months, under the direction of 66-year-old, eighteenth-generation president Kyuemon Hayakawa, workers remove the stones and the pressing lid from the vat, exposing the rich, fragrant miso that has long been treasured by emperors, shoguns, and common people alike.

AN HISTORIC LANDMARK

Hatcho Miso Company's rise to fame began in the late fifteenth century. Okazaki was the home of Japan's most famous warlord, Ieyasu Tokugawa, whose military exploits were popularized in the novel *Shogun*, by James Clavel. In the shadows of Tokugawa's castle, a small soybean miso shop supplied the vital ingredient for the shogun's power breakfast. Because of its concentrated nutrition and its ability to keep for years, Tokugawa's miso was one of his troops' most important military rations. After his army succeeded in conquering and unifying all of Japan, Tokugawa moved his headquarters to Tokyo and, until his death, ordered miso from his hometown miso shop. This official patronage as the "purveyor to the shogun" guaranteed Hatcho Miso Company the pre-eminence it still enjoys.

In 1892, Hatcho Miso Company received the even more prestigious honor of becoming the purveyor to the emperor of Japan. Today, busloads of tourists visit the 8th street shop to see where the famous miso of emperors and shoguns is made. However, you don't have to be a samurai or even live in Japan to enjoy hatcho miso. Since 1971, Mitoku Company has been exporting this same miso to natural foods distributors around the world.

Unlike other misos, which contain grains such as rice and barley, hatcho miso is made solely from whole soybeans and a minimum amount of water. A highly concentrated source of nutrition, hatcho miso also contains 80 percent more protein and 20 to 25 percent less salt than long-aged rice and barley misos.

Moreover, hatcho miso is a source of essential amino acids, minerals, and vitamins, and it is low in calories and fat. Hatcho miso has five times the fiber of an equal amount of celery.

MAKING HATCHO MISO

Although modern machines now do some of the work, the basic method at Hatcho Miso Company has changed little in the last 300 years. First, premium Hokkaido soybeans are washed and soaked in water for one hour. The beans are then transferred to a 2,000-pound-capacity cooker, steamed for two hours, then left in the closed cooker overnight. This unusual cooking process gives hatcho miso its deep, cocoa-brown color and characteristic smokey flavor.

The following morning, the soft, dark beans are crushed in a special machine that shapes them into two-inch crosses, allowing a greater surface area for the growth

A three-ton pyramid of stones tops each vat, pressing the miso.

of microorganisms. Next, the crosses are lightly dusted with a mixture of *Aspergillus* spores and toasted barley flour, then they are incubated for forty-eight hours under carefully controlled temperature and humidity. The "hatcho crosses"—now called koji—emerge from the incubation room covered with a fragrant bloom of pale yellow mold and loaded with powerful digestive enzymes. The koji is mixed with sea salt and a small amount of water and is then transferred to seven-foot-tall cedar vats. Each vat is covered with a thick cotton cloth and a heavy wooden pressing lid. A three-ton pyramid of stones tops the vats, pressing the miso. The unhurried process of natural aging begins. The enzymes supplied by the *Aspergillus* slowly mellow the mixture, transforming the complex protein, carbohydrates, and fats of the beans into dark, rich, flavorful amino and fatty acids and sweet simple sugars.

Finally, after at least two full years, the mature miso is scooped out with a wooden shovel. The best miso comes from deep down in the center of the vat. This was traditionally presented to Emperor Hirohito, who, until his recent death, enjoyed hatcho miso soup every day.

Although some manufacturers use the name hatcho miso for their dark soybean misos, only the special miso made since the 1300s on 8th Street in the small town of Okazaki is authentic hatcho miso. The exacting ancient process gives this miso its savory aroma, mellow sweetness, and astringent flavor. According to brewmaster Kazuo Kuroda, the extreme pressure of the stones on the dry miso creates a low-oxygen environment, which encourages the growth of hatcho's special type of bacteria. What's more, over the centuries, a particular strain of *Aspergillus* mold, known as *Aspergillus hatcho*, has made its home in the cracks and crevices of the old seasoned vats and throughout the fermentation rooms on Hatcho Street. *Aspergillus hatcho* gives this miso a unique flavor that has never been duplicated by other miso makers.

Hatcho miso is one of the few remaining traditionally made Japanese misos. After World War II, most miso manufacturers abandoned the expensive, lengthy natural aging in wood for less expensive, accelerated aging in temperature-controlled synthetic vats. Also, because hatcho miso is long-aged, contains little fermentable sugars, and is particularly dry, it is the only miso that can be packaged in sealed bags without pasteurization or added preservatives. Hatcho miso is a cultural artifact and, more than most Japanese foods, reflects the authentic taste of old Japan.

Hatcho miso and organic mellow hatcho miso (young, one-year-old hatcho miso) are available under the Mitoku Macrobiotic, Erewhon, Westbrae, and Tree of Life labels at better natural foods stores across America.

COOKING WITH HATCHO MISO

Like fine French wines, each miso has a distinct flavor, color, and aroma. Rich and savory, hatcho miso adds a harmonizing flavor and concentrated nutrition to a wide variety of dishes. For the busy cook who wants to add flavor and nutrition to standard American dishes, such as casseroles, gravies, chili, baked beans, and stews, simply substitute hatcho miso for salt (use approximately two tablespoons of miso for one teaspoon of salt). For those moving toward a more wholesome, natural way of eating, the hearty, meat-like quality of hatcho miso can help ease the transition. For example, try substituting vegetable stock seasoned with hatcho miso in recipes calling for beef stock. For the experienced cooks of natural foods, Japanese dishes, or gourmet fare, miso's possibilities are endless.

Hatcho miso's savory, robust flavor combines well with beans, gravies, baked and simmered dishes, and vegetable soups and stews. When making miso soup, combine one part hatcho miso with 2–3 parts light, sweet miso for an especially satisfying, balanced taste.

The Hatcho Miso Company, maker for five centuries of hatcho miso, the most revered miso in all Japan.

HATCHO MISO RECIPES

Sesame-Miso Dressing

Quick and easy, Sesame-Miso Dressing *adds rich flavor and nutrition to lightly steamed or blanched vegetables, especially green beans, broccoli, cauliflower, and leafy greens.*

2 tablespoons white or brown sesame seeds

2 teaspoons hatcho miso

1 tablespoon mirin

1 tablespoon rice syrup

1 teaspoon lemon juice

Yield: ⅓ cup

1. Toast sesame seeds in a dry skillet, stirring constantly over medium heat for approximately 2 minutes or just until seeds are fragrant or begin to pop. (Be careful not to over-toast, which causes bitterness.)

2. Grind seeds in a suribachi or mortar, add miso, and mix well. Add remaining ingredients and mix. The mixture will be thick and somewhat coarse.

3. Gently toss vegetables with mixture until evenly coated. Serve hot or at room temperature.

Udon in Sesame-Miso Broth

For a satisfying winter meal, serve this hearty and flavorful entrée piping hot, accompanied by a side dish of greens. In warmer weather, try omitting the sautéed vegetables, substitute 3 tablespoons white miso for the red miso, and top the noodles and broth with a colorful assortment of lightly steamed or simmered vegetables.

1 tablespoon sesame oil
2 slices fresh ginger root
$\frac{1}{2}$ cup thinly sliced onion
$\frac{1}{2}$ cup sliced celery
$\frac{2}{3}$ cup sliced carrots
4 cups stock or water
$\frac{1}{3}$ cup sesame seeds, toasted
2 level tablespoons hatcho miso
2 level tablespoons red (rice) miso
1 tablespoon mirin
1 pound uncooked udon
Slivered scallions for garnish

Serves: 4–5

1. Heat oil in medium-sized pot. Sauté ginger until golden brown, then discard.

2. Sauté onion until translucent. Add celery and carrots, and sauté briefly. Add stock or water, and bring to a boil. Reduce heat, cover, and simmer until vegetables are tender.

3. While vegetables are cooking, thoroughly grind toasted seeds in a suribachi or mortar. Add the misos, mirin, and $\frac{1}{2}$ cup of broth. Purée with seeds, then add to soup.

4. Cook udon in 4–5 quarts of rapidly boiling water until just al dente (firm). Drain, rinse briefly in a cold water bath, and drain again. Divide noodles in 4 or 5 bowls.

5. Ladle hot miso broth over top of noodles to almost cover. Garnish with scallions and serve.

▶ *Nobuo Kamata unearths a giant kuzu root.*

▼ *Brewmaster Toshio Sumiya mixes a batch of fermenting mirin.*

▲ At the Onozaki Miso Shop, Itsuko Onozaki places developing koji in wooden trays to be incubated overnight.

▶ Workers at the Hatcho Miso Company place the last few stones on a six-ton vat of hatcho miso.

◀ *Sweet rice mochi is spread out in sheets to dry and harden.*

▼ *Yoshiaki Sakurai hangs whole wheat udon to slowly dry in the Sakurai Noodle Shop.*

▲ Shiitake farmer Norio Watanabe drills holes into an oak log for shiitake spawn.

▲ Workers at Watanabe Shiitake Farm hammer shiitake spawn into the logs.

▲ The growing shiitake.

▲ Shiitake ready for harvest.

▲ Sachiko Watanabe picks shiitake.

Miso Gravy

Nothing raises interest in basic grain dishes such as millet, rice, and polenta like a tasty gravy. This gravy also goes well with seitan cutlets, tempeh, and other vegetarian favorites.

1 ½ tablespoons sesame or olive oil

1–2 cloves garlic, finely minced

1 onion, diced

3 tablespoons whole wheat or unbleached wheat flour

1 ½ cups vegetable stock, Dashi *(page 105)*, or water

2 teaspoons hatcho miso

¼ teaspoon sea salt

¼ teaspoon dried basil

1 tablespoon mirin or sake

2–3 tablespoons minced fresh parsley

Yield: 1 ½ cups

1. In a saucepan, sauté garlic and onion over medium-low heat until translucent.

2. Add flour, and stir constantly 1 minute. Slowly add stock or water while stirring briskly. Stir frequently until gravy simmers and begins to thicken.

3. Thin miso in 1 tablespoon water and add to pan along with salt, basil, mirin or sake, and parsley.

4. Simmer gently, uncovered, 10–15 minutes, stirring occasionally. Keep warm until ready to use.

Miso Rice Pilaf

Fluffy, flavorful, and highly nutritious, Miso Rice Pilaf is an excellent way to introduce brown rice to those who are unfamiliar with natural foods. The basic method (below) is for pressure cooking this dish. For pot-boiling the pilaf, see variation.

2–3 dried shiitake
4 cups water
4-inch piece kombu
3 cups uncooked brown rice
4 level tablespoons hatcho, red (rice), or barley miso
⅓ cup minced onion
⅓ cup minced celery
1 bay leaf
⅔ cup minced fresh parsley

Serves: 6

1. In a pressure cooker, soak shiitake in water for 20-30 minutes. Next, add kombu and bring to a simmer, uncovered, over medium heat. As soon as water begins to simmer, remove kombu and reserve for another use. Mince shiitake and return to stock.

2. While kombu is coming to a simmer, wash the rice and drain well. Roast the rice in an unoiled skillet over medium heat, stirring constantly until golden and fragrant.

3. Dissolve miso in some of the broth, then return it to the pot along with onion, celery, and bay leaf. Bring to a boil and slowly add roasted rice. Allow to boil 1 minute then cover, bring to pressure, and cook 45 minutes.

4. Remove from heat and allow pressure to return to normal before uncovering.

5. Add parsley, toss well, and cover. Let sit for 10 minutes before serving. Garnish with sprig of parsley.

VARIATION

- Try adding sautéed onion or shallots and some chopped walnuts to the cooked rice. Then use this delicious variation in stuffed peppers or squash.

- If pot-boiling, use a heavy pot with a tight-fitting lid for best results. Use 6 cups water and add an extra tablespoon of miso. Boil over low heat 40 minutes, then reduce to very low and cook 20 minutes more. Do not remove cover while cooking.

4

MOCHI

The Sweet Rice Treat

Mochi, a delicious whole grain food, is made from a glutinous, high-protein variety of rice called sweet rice. The sweet rice is soaked, steamed, and pounded; then it is allowed to dry until it is firm enough to slice.

Late in December, traditional Japanese villages resound with the rhythmic pounding of sweet rice as families prepare mochi for the festive New Year's meal. A large, smooth bowl—made from a hollowed-out log carved generations before— and a heavy wooden mallet are set in place as the annual mochi-pounding ritual begins. It is usually the grandmother who begins the tradition by placing steamed rice into the hollowed log. After each resonant stroke of the grandfather's mallet, the grandmother turns the rice. They work together quickly and rhythmically. Grandmother bobs in, turns the mound, then leans aside each time the mallet crashes down, releasing billows of steam from the hot rice.

After being pounded into a homogenous mass, the mochi is formed into small, flat cakes or balls known as *o-hagi*. Coated with sesame seeds or ground nuts, o-hagi is a children's favorite. The remaining mochi is allowed to dry, then it is stored in a cold place or refrigerated for later use.

Mochi can be prepared in a variety of ways to become the focal point of a meal. Naturally sweet and filling, this sweet rice food is also an ideal between-meal snack. Physically strengthening and easy to digest, mochi is an excellent food for people who are in a weakened condition. Japanese farmers and laborers favor mochi during colder months because of its reputation for increasing one's stamina.

Mochi is recommended for such health problems as anemia, blood-sugar imbalances, and weak intestines. Pregnant and lactating women benefit, for it strengthens both mother and child and encourages a plentiful supply of milk. Mochi made with the herb mugwort, which grows wild throughout Japan, is particularly high in calcium and iron and is traditionally given to women after childbirth. Mugwort mochi is also good for people who are anemic.

Although mochi is still hand-pounded for the holidays, most of the pure white mochi found in Japanese supermarkets and Oriental foods stores in the United States is squeezed through a modern grinder/extruder. Pounding mochi is back-breaking work, but mochi produced this way is significantly better tasting than the extruded product. What's more, some traditionalists feel extruded mochi lacks the healing qualities of the traditional pounded variety. Fortunately, there are a few small mochi makers that combine the quality of pounding with the convenience of automation. One of these is Nobuyuki Kojima, maker of Mitoku Company's organic sweet brown rice mochi.

AUTHENTIC MOCHI MAKER

Born and raised in Nagoya, in a family of grain dealers, Nobuyuki Kojima has worked with rice all his life. As a young man, one of his family responsibilities was milling the bran from brown rice to make white rice. He always looked forward to running his father's business.

However, at the age of twenty-three, Kojima was afflicted with a debilitating kidney disease that left him bedridden for six months. Totally discouraged with modern medicine and desperate to find some relief, he discharged himself from the hospital and immediately started a twenty-day fast. Using various traditional healing practices, such as acupuncture, herbal medicine, and yoga, Kojima slowly began to regain his strength.

Ironically, one day after Kojima returned to his rice-milling responsibilities, a customer happened to ask for whole grain brown rice. Kojima was shocked. Over the past one-hundred years, highly polished rice had become a staple throughout

Japan. "What are you going to do with brown rice?" asked Kojima. "I am going to eat it for my health," the elderly man laughingly replied. The customer went on to tell Kojima that brown rice had been recommended to him for his heart condition by a macrobiotic teacher. Moreover, he reported that eating brown rice every day had greatly improved his general health.

That conversation, which took place over twenty-five years ago, literally transformed Kojima's life. Not only did he begin eating brown rice, which greatly improved his health, but in 1974 he started making brown rice mochi. At that time, making mochi from anything other than pure-white sweet rice was almost unheard of.

MAKING BROWN RICE MOCHI

Presently, Kojima makes thousands of pounds of brown rice mochi every month, using methods he has developed through the years. His seven-day process begins by steaming 1,200 pounds of sweet brown rice, which yields about 1,600 pounds of mochi. The steamed rice is passed through a grinder that is similar to, but much larger than, the hand grinder used to chop meat. Grinding changes the whole grains of sweet brown rice into a sticky dough.

Next, the sweet-rice dough is pounded about sixty times by a uniquely designed automatic pounding machine. During the pounding stage, individual grains of rice are further broken down until they form a smooth, sticky mass. Kojima feels this hard pounding is what gives mochi its concentrated energy.

After pounding, while the mochi is still warm and soft, it is placed in molding boxes to set. The boxes are then placed in a refrigerator for three days.

The chilled mochi is cut easily into small blocks (approximately 1 x 2 inches). To prevent spoilage, Kojima immediately vacuum-packs his mochi and then sterilizes it by using steam heat. The complex packaging process gives Kojima's mochi a one-year shelf life and enables him to ship his product around the world.

In Japan, as well as North America, Kojima's most popular mochi is made with 100 percent organic sweet brown rice. However, he also makes other types of mochi by adding millet, mugwort, or black sesame seeds to the sweet brown rice.

A word of caution: it is possible to eat too much mochi, especially Kojima's mochi. Mochi has a way of growing in your stomach. Oddly, in Japan the antidote for eating too much mochi is more rice! *Nanakusa* (seven herbs of spring), which is a simple rice gruel cooked with seven herbs, is often served around the holidays to relieve a bloated stomach. However, we've discovered that the best way to survive a mochi feast is with a long walk.

COOKING WITH MOCHI

Mochi is versatile and easy to cook. Once pounded, shaped, and dried until firm, mochi can be baked, broiled, grilled, pan-fried, or deep-fried. When prepared using any of these methods, mochi puffs up to nearly double its size, developing a crisp exterior and a soft, melting interior. If cooked too long, the surface will crack and the soft inside part will ooze out. So watch mochi carefully while it cooks.

Baked, broiled, or grilled mochi is often eaten with a sweet miso topping. Baked mochi can also be cut into bite-sized pieces and added to soups during the last minute of cooking. Pan- or deep-fried mochi needs nothing more than a light seasoning of soy sauce or a soy sauce and ginger-based dip. Mochi can also be rolled in rice syrup, then coated with walnut meal and eaten as dessert. Melt a couple pieces of mochi in a waffle iron, then top the delicious whole grain waffle with warmed rice syrup and chopped, toasted pecans or walnuts.

Soaking excessively dry mochi for several hours in cold water will cause it to soften. It can then be prepared in any way.

After being pounded for several minutes, the mochi is removed from the hollow log.

MOCHI RECIPES

Pan-Fried Mochi

1 teaspoon toasted sesame oil
6 pieces mochi (2 x 2 ½ inches)

Serves: 2

1. Heat oil in a large skillet. Add mochi and cook, covered, over low heat until mochi bottoms are slightly browned (about 5 minutes).

2. Flip mochi pieces, add 1–2 teaspoons water to create steam and to soften mochi, cover again, and cook a few minutes more. Remove cover as soon as mochi is cooked (to prevent mochi from melting).

3. Cooked mochi is often served with a shoyu and ginger-based dip. It can also be rolled in a mixture of equal parts shoyu and water, then wrapped in strips of toasted nori.

Broiled Mochi

In Japan, broiled or grilled mochi is often served with a sweet miso topping such as the one suggested here. It can also be served in the ways suggested for Pan-Fried Mochi *(page 57).*

¼ cup mellow white miso, or 2 tablespoons red (rice) miso

1 tablespoon lemon juice

2 tablespoons rice malt

1 tablespoon mirin

1 rounded tablespoon tahini

1 teaspoon fresh ginger juice

2 tablespoons water

12 pieces mochi (2 x 2 ½ inches)

Serves: 4

1. To prepare sweet miso topping, combine and mix first seven ingredients in a suribachi or small bowl.

2. Place mochi pieces on oiled cookie sheet or broiling pan. Broil on both sides until mochi is slightly puffed and the outside is crisp and golden. (Watch carefully to prevent overcooking.)

3. Spread thin layer of sweet miso topping on each mochi piece and broil 1 minute more. Topping should be slightly browned but not burned. Serve immediately.

Deep-Fried Mochi in Broth

Deep-fried mochi is delicious when served with a dip or wrapped in toasted nori strips, but we like it best when it is served in broth.

2 cups Dashi *(page 105)* or Kombu Stock *(page 170)*
2 $\frac{1}{2}$–3 tablespoons shoyu
2 tablespoons mirin
Vegetable oil for deep-frying
9 pieces mochi (2 x 2 $\frac{1}{2}$ inches)
$\frac{1}{3}$ cup finely grated daikon
Minced scallion for garnish

Serves: 3

1. Prepare stock. Add shoyu and mirin and simmer briefly. Keep hot (not boiling).

2. In a pot, heat 2 inches oil to 325°F (until a drop of flour-water batter sinks to bottom of the pot and immediately rises to the surface).

3. Gently place mochi, 2–3 pieces at a time, into oil and fry, turning occasionally until the outside is crisp and golden. Drain on absorbent paper. Continue until all mochi is fried.

4. In individual serving bowls, place 2 pieces of mochi on the bottom and 1 piece on top to form a pyramid. Pour about $\frac{1}{2}$ cup hot broth over mochi, and top with 2 tablespoons grated daikon and a sprinkle of scallion.

Mochi Soup (O-zoni)

Symbolizing longevity and wealth in Japan, mochi is traditionally included in the first meal of the New Year, usually in soup or stew.

8 cups Dashi *(page 105)* or Kombu Stock *(page 170)*
1 burdock root
1 large carrot
$\frac{1}{2}$ teaspoon sea salt
8 fresh shiitake or white mushrooms, sliced
1 tablespoon mirin
3 scallions, trimmed and cut in 1-inch lengths
4 Chinese cabbage leaves (or other tender greens), chopped
6 pieces mochi (2 x 2 $\frac{1}{2}$ inches)
$\frac{1}{4}$–$\frac{1}{3}$ cup mellow white miso (to taste), or 2 tablespoons shoyu

Serves: 5-6

1. Prepare stock.

2. Scrub burdock, cut in 2-inch-long julienne strips and immediately place in cold water to prevent discoloration. Cut carrot similarly but a little thicker.

3. Drain burdock and add to stock along with salt. Simmer 10–15 minutes, then add carrots and mushrooms. (If dried shiitake are used, they must be soaked and stemmed before slicing.) Simmer 10 minutes.

4. Add mirin, scallions, and cabbage. Cook 5 minutes more.

5. While soup is cooking, cut the mochi squares into bite-sized pieces and place on lightly oiled cookie sheet. Bake at 350°F until slightly brown and puffy. (Check frequently to avoid overcooking.) Remove and set aside.

6. When cabbage is just tender, add mochi and shoyu (if using), and gently simmer 1 minute more.

7. Dissolve miso in a little of the broth before adding it to soup.

8. Let soup sit 1–2 minutes before serving.

Sweet Pecan Mochi

Sweet Pecan Mochi is a delicious and satisfying dessert, snack, or special breakfast treat.

1 cup pecan halves
$\frac{1}{8}$ teaspoon sea salt
8 pieces mochi (2 x 2 $\frac{1}{2}$ inches)
$\frac{1}{3}$ cup rice malt

Serves: 4

1. In a dry skillet over medium heat, toast the pecans, stirring constantly until crisp and fragrant (3–5 minutes).

2. Transfer pecans to a bowl or suribachi, and grind into a coarse meal. Add salt, toss well, and taste. Add more salt, if desired. Set aside.

3. Pan-fry the mochi (page 57). When tender, dip each piece in rice malt to coat. (If malt is too thick, warm it until it flows easily.) Shake off excess malt, then roll pieces in generous amount of roasted pecan meal. Enjoy!

5
NOODLES
Traditional Japanese Fare

D uring the hot, humid summers around Japan's picturesque ancient capital of Kyoto, one can still experience *nagashi somen*, the epitome of cooling and relaxing summer fare. From the kitchen, chilled, ultra-fine and silky smooth somen noodles are sent down a long bamboo chute into a stream of clear, cold spring water in the beautifully landscaped garden where guests sit, perhaps under a cool bamboo thicket. As the noodles lazily float past, guests fish them out with chopsticks and dip them in a chilled broth.

More noodles are probably eaten in Japan today than any other food except rice. Light and easy to digest, quick and simple to prepare, delicious and satisfying, Japanese eggless noodles are a versatile food. They make a filling lunch, convenient snack, or, when served with one or two side dishes, a complete dinner. During the heat of summer, noodles are deliciously refreshing when served floating in a bowl of ice water and accompanied by a chilled dipping sauce. For warmth in the winter, noodles are commonly served in piping hot broth. Whether in soups or salads, sautéed with vegetables, deep-fried, baked, or topped with sauce, noodles are delicious. Quick to prepare, they provide the perfect solution when you have unexpected guests or find yourself at mealtime with nothing "in the works." In the time it takes for the water to boil and the noodles to cook, you can prepare a broth or sauce and a vegetable dish and voilà! In twenty minutes you can create a nutritious and satisfying meal.

Although there are many varieties within each group, there are two main types of Japanese noodles: those made from buckwheat (soba) and those made from wheat (udon and somen). Since buckwheat requires cooler, drier growing conditions, the thin brownish-gray soba noodle is most popular in northern Japan. Udon, a thick, chewy beige wheat noodle, is favored in Kyoto and southern Japan. In winter, both types are most often enjoyed in hot broth either plain or topped with simmered vegetables. In the summer, soba is commonly eaten cold with a chilled dipping sauce, but southerners prefer either hiyamugi or somen—thin, vermicelli-type wheat noodles—in the summer. Traditionally, udon is not served cold. See inset *Versatile Japanese Noodles* beginning on page 66 for more information.

The Japanese feel that their traditional "fast food" must be eaten immediately, before the piping hot broth has made the noodles limp. The slurping sounds that result can be strange to Western ears, but it is a sign of enjoyment in Japan. In fact, eating noodles slowly and quietly is offensive to the cook. On the first day of our trip to Japan we were taken to a "noodle bar" for lunch. The sound of fifty or more businessmen all slurping noodles at once is something we will never forget!

Noodle bars abound in Japanese cities, and many of them still offer *te-uchi* (hand-made) soba and udon. At the window of a steamy little noodle shop one cannot help but be fascinated by the sight of a Japanese chef kneading and slicing fresh pasta dough, the noodles rolling in a cauldron of boiling water, and a variety of tempting noodle dishes being served to eager customers. This is a rare instance when—unless you make your own noodles—you can actually get something better in a restaurant than at home.

THE MAKING OF AUTHENTIC HAND-MADE NOODLES

Although you simply cannot beat the fresh taste and texture of professionally made te-uchi noodles, there is a family in the foothills of the Japanese Alps that makes soba and udon in the simple, uncomplicated way that duplicates the hand-made process. If you have tasted Erewhon, Tree of Life, Macro Pasta, and Mitoku noodles, then you have had a hint of that hand-made taste. These brands are all made at the Sakurai Noodle Shop in Monokamo City, Gifu, Japan. However, to experience the authentic te-uchi taste, try the thick organic soba and udon made by the Sakurai family for the Mitoku Macrobiotic label.

The Sakurais' traditional process begins by adding sea-salt brine to freshly stone-ground organic flour. The correct salt content is critical for developing the right amount of gluten in the dough and for insurance against rancidity. The dough is thoroughly mixed and kneaded, then allowed to rest to develop the gluten.

After several hours, the dough is checked for the correct level of "stickiness." It is then passed through a series of rollers to form thin, long, continuous sheets. The last roller has a cutter attached, which can be changed to cut the dough into either thin *ito* (thread) soba and somen or thick traditional udon or soba noodles. Whether thick or thin, the long strands emerging from the cutter are chopped into six-foot sections and carried to a special drying room.

Not willing to compromise quality—like his grandfather—company head Yoshiaki Sakurai still hangs his noodles over bamboo rods to dry at natural temperatures. Fans are employed in the drying rooms to keep the air circulating. Artificial heat, common in modern processing to speed up the drying process, is not used because it adversely affects quality. From start to finish, the Sakurai family's methods are based on the way noodles are made at home.

After drying for at least thirty hours, the noodles are cut into shorter lengths for packaging. The whole process takes about four times as long as the modern process, which can be completed in an eight-hour day. Although his company is large enough to afford a modern packing machine, Yoshiaki turns the tedious task of hand packing his product into a social event. Local farmers' wives, sitting on their knees, chatting and laughing as they work, quickly and efficiently weigh noodles, then slide them into long, slender bags.

Ramen is not considered a Japanese noodle. The ramen that Americans know is a modern version of Chinese-style noodles served hot in a rich broth containing various vegetables, meat, or fish. Most modern commercial types of ramen are made by first frying and then oven-drying the noodles. To avoid the problem of rancidity, the oil used must contain preservatives such as BHT (butylated hydroxytoluene). In association with Mitoku, the Sakurai family was the first to introduce a natural whole wheat ramen by the "steam-then-bake" method. Since then, there has been a great demand for this ramen, which is found in an assortment of flavors and varieties. Sakurai's steam-bake ramens are those found under the Westbrae, Soba Shop, Erewhon, and Tree of Life labels.

It's not just the time-consuming natural process that makes Sakurai organic noodles and ramen special; it is also their extraordinary ingredients. The fresh flour used is stone-ground each morning at the Sakurai shop and is grown by a unique agricultural method known as nature farming. While most grain growers use modern chemical methods, Sakurai's farmers do not use synthetic fertilizers, animal manures, herbicides, or pesticides. Nature farming stresses the importance of building the vitality of the topsoil by adding mulch made from locally available plant

Versatile Japanese Noodles

Udon

A thick, cream-colored wheat noodle, udon resembles linguine. High-quality udon noodles are made from 100 percent whole wheat flour or a combination of whole wheat and unbleached white flour. One-hundred percent whole wheat udon is a sturdy noodle with a full whole wheat flavor. There are other lighter, smoother udons that readily absorb the flavors of broths, sauces, and seasonings. Brown rice udon (a combination of brown rice flour and wheat flour) was developed for the natural foods market.

Though usually served in broth or with a strong-flavored dipping sauce, udon is also good when pan-fried. It can be used in noodle salads as well. Easy to prepare, udon is ideal when on the road or camping.

Soba

Several varieties of soba are available at natural foods stores. One-hundred percent buckwheat soba is a hearty, delicious wheat-free noodle. It must be cooked more gently to minimize breaking, so frying is not recommended.

Most soba noodles are made from 40–60 percent buckwheat flour with the remainder being unbleached white flour. Ito soba, which is 40 percent buckwheat flour, is a thin, delicate noodle, which cooks quickly and easily absorbs the flavor of broth, sauces, or seasonings. Like cha soba (made with the addition of green-tea powder), ito soba is especially good served cold in the summer. Yomogi (mugwort) soba, another special variety, contains mineral-rich dried mugwort leaves. Mugwort soba, cha soba, and ito soba are not recommended for frying. Jinenjo soba is another popular noodle in Japan. A strengthening food rich in digestive enzymes, jinenjo helps bind the buckwheat flour, resulting in a smooth, soft noodle that is excellent in broth, yet sturdy enough for frying. Noodles that are 80 percent soba, 50 percent soba, and 40 percent soba all have a rich flavor and substantial texture. They may be used in any of the soba recipes presented in this chapter.

Somen

Whole wheat somen is a thin, light noodle that is traditionally served cold. Somen cooks quickly and absorbs the flavor of sauces, dressings, and seasonings well, so it is both convenient and versatile. Try tossing cooked somen with a variety of raw or parboiled vegetables then top with your favorite salad dressing (miso or umeboshi-based dressings go particularly well). These delicate noodles are also delicious served with a hot miso broth or a shoyu-flavored dipping sauce (hot or chilled) that has been garnished with minced scallions, slivered nori, and grated ginger. A sweet and sour vegetable or tofu sauce is excellent served over somen. For an elegant entrée, try somen in Noodle Rolls (page 74). Whole wheat somen can be substituted for white somen in Oriental recipes, but it requires slightly longer cooking.

Ramen

Natural ramen is a quick-cooking, tasty convenience food. It is available in whole wheat and in blends of whole wheat, buckwheat or brown rice flour, and unbleached white flour. Ramen is sold with or without flavor packets, which are added to the cooking water to make an instant broth. A wide range of flavors, including curry, spicy szechuan, mushroom, and ginger-tamari, are available. If you buy ramen plain, cook and drain the noodles, and immediately serve them in Dashi (page 105) topped with a garnish of slivered scallions.

materials. In this naturally balanced environment, grains and vegetables thrive without the use of agricultural chemicals.

The Sakurai family's dedication to quality and tradition dates back to the fifteenth century when their ancestors began grain farming. In 1911, Seiichi Sakurai started making noodles. Around 1960, the Sakurai family joined a religious group that advocated natural agriculture and traditional manufacturing. By the 1970s, the efforts of the Sakurai family paid off as they gained recognition as producers of Japan's highest-quality noodles. Today, Sakurai noodles and ramen can be found under several different labels on the shelves of natural foods stores on five continents. However, the current company president, Yoshiaki, is not satisfied with making only Oriental noodles. Although, he admits, his great-grandfather would probably not approve, in 1986 the Sakurai Noodle Company began making organic spaghetti and macaroni for the Japanese natural foods market. What would Marco Polo think?

COOKING JAPANESE NOODLES

Since most Japanese noodles are made with salt, it is not necessary or advisable to add salt to the cooking water. In a large pot, bring the water (about ten cups of water for every eight ounces of noodles) to a full rolling boil. Add the noodles a few at a time so as not to completely stop the boiling. Stir gently until the water is boiling rapidly again to prevent the noodles from sticking to the bottom of the pan. If too many noodles are added at once, the water will not quickly return to a boil and the noodles will be overcooked on the outside and undercooked on the inside. Also, using too little water will result in sticky, unevenly cooked noodles.

There are two acceptable methods for cooking noodles. The first method is quite basic. Simply bring the water in the pot back to a rapid boil once all the noodles have been added (as just described), then cook the noodles over medium heat until done. The second method is known as the "shock method." Once the noodles have been added to the pot and the water returns to a rolling boil, a cup of cold water is added to "shock" the noodles. When the water returns to a boil again, another cup of cold water is added. This is repeated three or four times until the noodles are cooked. No matter which method is used, noodles should be tested often to avoid overcooking. A properly cooked noodle should be slightly chewy. When broken in half, the noodle should be the same color throughout.

Once cooked, immediately drain and rinse the noodles in two or three cold-water baths or under cold running water to prevent further cooking and to keep the noodles from sticking together. When they have cooled enough to handle, and while still in the cold bath or under running water, gently rub the noodles between your hands to remove any surface starch. Drain and set aside until ready to assemble your dish. If reheating is necessary, place individual noodles in a strainer or colander and submerge in a pot of boiling water until just heated. Drain well and serve.

The noodle cooking water can be reserved, allowed to sour slightly, and can then be used as a natural leavening agent in breads, muffins, and pancakes.

NOODLE RECIPES

Noodles in Broth

This popular, satisfying dish takes little time to prepare. Simply served with a garnish of scallion, Noodles in Broth makes a filling lunch or a substitute for soup in a heartier meal. You can top the noodles with a colorful assortment of steamed, simmered, or deep-fried vegetables; fish; tofu; mochi; or seitan for a complete dinner. Udon or soba are recommended.

3 cups Dashi *(page 105)*
8 ounces uncooked udon or soba
$\frac{1}{8}$ teaspoon sea salt
2 tablespoons tamari or shoyu
1 $\frac{1}{2}$ tablespoons mirin
1–2 teaspoons fresh ginger juice
Finely minced scallion for garnish

Serves: 2

1. Cook noodles (see page 68 for cooking methods).

2. Prepare *Dashi* in a medium-sized pot. Add salt, tamari or shoyu, and mirin. Simmer 1 minute. Remove from heat and add ginger juice.

3. To serve, divide noodles in deep individual serving bowls. Ladle hot broth over noodles to almost cover, and garnish with minced scallion or topping of choice.

Summer Soba

Cool and refreshing when little else appeals, this traditional noodle dish is a favorite Japanese lunch on a hot summer day. Light, delicate soba varieties such as ito, cha, and mugwort soba are especially appealing. Whole wheat somen noodles are a good substitute.

3 cups Dashi *(page 105)*
$\frac{1}{8}$ teaspoon sea salt
3 tablespoons tamari or shoyu
2 tablespoons mirin
8 ounces uncooked soba

CONDIMENTS
1 teaspoon wasabi powder *(Japanese horseradish)*, optional
1 teaspoon peeled and finely grated ginger root
$\frac{1}{4}$ sheet toasted nori, broken into bite-sized pieces
3 tablespoons minced scallions

Serves: 2

1. Prepare stock in a medium-sized pot. Add salt, tamari or shoyu, and mirin. Simmer 1 minute, remove from heat, and refrigerate.

2. Cook noodles (see page 68 for cooking methods).

3. Add one drop of water at a time to wasabi and mix until it forms a thick paste. Prepare other condiments.

4. Divide cooked noodles into small noodle baskets, plates, or soup bowls. (If noodles stick together, rinse under cold water and drain well before serving.)

5. Pour chilled dipping broth into small individual bowls. Set out prepared wasabi, ginger, nori, and scallion in separate bowls so they can be added to the broth according to individual tastes. (About 2 teaspoons scallion and $\frac{1}{8}$ teaspoon wasabi or ginger is recommended for every $\frac{1}{2}$-$\frac{2}{3}$ cup broth.)

6. Dip each bite of noodles in chilled broth. If dip becomes weak, replace with fresh broth.

Japanese-Style "Fried" Noodles

In this tasty Japanese dish, cooked noodles are simply tossed in a pan with sautéed vegetables and a small amount of sweet and savory sauce. Mirin and mellow miso combine for a perfect marriage of flavors. Minced scallion adds color as well as fresh crispness.

8 ounces uncooked udon
2 ½ tablespoons mellow white or sweet white miso
2 ½ tablespoons mirin
1 tablespoon light or toasted sesame oil
2 tablespoons minced shallot or 2 cloves garlic, finely minced
Minced scallion for garnish

Serves: 2–3

1. Cook noodles (see page 68 for cooking methods).

2. Combine miso and mirin in a small bowl.

3. Heat oil in a large skillet, add minced shallot or garlic, and sauté over medium-low heat 1 minute. (Be careful not to brown garlic or it will become bitter.)

4. Add miso-mirin mixture to the skillet, then add noodles and toss to evenly coat. (It may be necessary to add a little water.) Sauté 1 minute more, then remove from heat.

5. Serve immediately with generous sprinkling of scallion.

Spicy Soba Salad

Vary the vegetables according to availability. Fresh peas, corn, red and green bell pepper, and radishes are good, colorful options.

8 ounces soba

1 large or 2 medium carrots, cut into $1\frac{1}{2}$-inch matchsticks

$1\frac{1}{2}$ cups broccoli florets

2 scallions, slivered

2 tablespoons minced parsley

DRESSING

1 tablespoon light sesame oil

1 tablespoon toasted sesame oil

$\frac{1}{4}$ teaspoon chili-flavored sesame oil*

2 tablespoons tamari or shoyu

$\frac{1}{4}$ teaspoon sea salt

3 tablespoons brown rice vinegar

1 clove garlic, finely minced

Serves: 3–4

1. Break noodles into 3 or 4 even lengths and cook (see page 68 for cooking methods).

2. Parboil carrots and broccoli for 2 minutes, rinse under cold water, and drain well. Combine all vegetables with cooked noodles in a medium-sized bowl.

3. Whisk dressing ingredients together and add to noodle mixture. Toss gently and serve.

---

*Chili-flavored sesame oil is available in most well-stocked natural foods stores, Asian food stores, and some specialty shops and supermarkets.

Noodles With Miso-Tahini Sauce

Udon and whole wheat somen go especially well with this popular sauce, but soba can be substituted with good results. This recipe is one of our family favorites and a great choice when you need a quick and easy meal for unexpected guests. The recipe below is simply garnished with scallion. For a heartier version, top the noodles and sauce with a colorful assortment of steamed vegetables.

8 ounces uncooked udon or whole wheat somen

4 level tablespoons mellow white miso

3–4 tablespoons tahini

$\frac{1}{3}$ cup water

2 tablespoons brown rice vinegar or lemon juice

1 tablespoon mirin

$1\frac{1}{2}$–2 teaspoons fresh ginger juice

1 clove garlic, finely minced

Pinch dried tarragon or thyme (optional)

Minced scallion for garnish

Serves: 2–3

1. Cook noodles (see page 68 for cooking methods).

2. Combine miso and tahini in a saucepan. Add water, a little at a time, and mix well to form a smooth sauce.

3. Add remaining ingredients and bring just to a simmer. If too thick, add a little more water; if too thin, simmer briefly to thicken.

4. To serve, place noodles in individual serving bowls, spoon sauce over top, and garnish with scallion.

Noodle Rolls

Noodle rolls require a delicate hand but are not difficult to make. When patiently and skillfully prepared, the reward is a beautiful, elegant, and tasty main dish. For variety, add other ingredients with the noodles to fill the rolls. Strips of fried tempeh or seitan, sauerkraut, blanched scallion greens, radish sprouts, and toasted and ground sesame seeds are excellent filling choices.

8 ounces uncooked thin soba or whole wheat somen

4 sheets nori

$1-1\frac{1}{2}$ teaspoons wasabi powder (Japanese horseradish)

DIPPING SAUCE
$1\frac{1}{2}$ tablespoons shoyu
$1\frac{1}{2}$ tablespoons water or soup stock
$1\frac{1}{2}$ teaspoons mirin (optional)

Serves: 4

1. Cook noodles (see page 68 for cooking directions).

2. Once drained, neatly arrange noodles on a clean, dry towel. Spread them out in even lines from left to right.

3 Toast nori (directions on page 179). Place one sheet of nori, toasted side down, on a sushi mat, small towel, or counter. Lay one quarter of the noodles side by side across the nori. (There should be $\frac{1}{2}$ inch of uncovered nori at the bottom and the top.) Roll up nori as firmly as possible. Let the roll rest on its seam.

4. Repeat with remaining sheets of nori and noodles.

5. Using a sharp knife (and cleaning the blade after each cut), carefully slice rolls in half, then cut each half into 3 equal pieces.

6. Make dipping sauce by combining shoyu, water or stock, and mirin in a small bowl. Place in small individual saucers.

7. Add one drop of water at a time to wasabi, and mix until it forms a thick paste.

8. To serve, place noodle roll pieces, cut side up, on a platter along with mound of wasabi paste. Add wasabi to individual bowls of dipping sauce. Wasabi is strong-flavored, so begin by adding a small amount to sauce, then add more depending on individual taste.

6

RICE MALT

Heavenly Sweet Water

S ugars are the fuel of life and sweeteners are something everyone instinctively desires. How we satisfy this craving for sweets can have a significant effect on our health and happiness. The quick energy lift from refined white sugar, brown sugar, fructose, honey, and maple syrup can cause rapid mood shifts on a daily basis. Over long periods of time, this can result in mental illness, hypoglycemia, diabetes, and other hormonal and degenerative diseases.

When choosing sweeteners, it is important to consider both quantity and quality. There is, of course, a world of difference between using lots of white sugar, which has no nutritional value, and using a moderate amount of honey or maple syrup, which has some nutritional value. However, even regular consumption of these higher-quality sweeteners can cause rapid upsurges in blood-sugar levels, followed soon after by dramatic plummets. This cycle, often referred to as the "sugar blues," is due to a high concentration of simple sugars. The next time you start the day with pancakes smothered in maple syrup, pay particular attention to your emotions over the next few hours. The first sign of the sugar blues is usually anxiety or irritability, typically followed by low energy or depression.

If you are eating a healing diet or if you simply want to enjoy the highest-quality sweeteners available, choose naturally malted whole grain sweeteners such as rice and brown rice malt. Like many of the traditional foods discussed in this book, rice malt is made by a slow, natural enzymatic process, as the whole grains are partially broken down to yield a thick, rich, sweet liquid.

Rice malt contains about 30 percent soluble complex carbohydrates, 45 percent maltose (grain-malt sugar), 3–4 percent glucose, and 20 percent water. The glucose is absorbed into the blood almost immediately. The maltose takes up to one and a half hours to digest, and the complex carbohydrates are gradually digested and released for up to four hours. Unlike other concentrated sweeteners, which are high in simple sugars, rice malt provides a slow but prolonged source of energy that is calming and soothing.

Another advantage of rice or brown rice malt is that it has many of the B vitamins and minerals that are found in rice and sprouted barley. Characteristically rich but mild flavored, rice malt complements simple foods, whereas honey, maple syrup, and molasses have stronger, often overpowering tastes.

Before Commodore Perry's ships forced open Japan's ports to American trade almost 140 years ago, the Japanese sweet tooth was usually satisfied with the subtle sweetness of amazake (fermented sweet rice pudding), mirin (sweet rice wine), or brown rice malt. Today, after over a century of experimenting with white sugar, the Japanese are also singing the "sugar blues." But scattered throughout Japan are a few small traditional shops that still make rice and brown rice malt exactly the way it was made before the introduction of white sugar.

PRESERVING AUTHENTIC BROWN RICE MALT

In ancient times, rice malt was believed to be of divine origin. As if by some heavenly plan, the addition of a few sprouts of barley to rice resulted in golden liquid sweetness. Rice was considered a gift of the gods, and its transformation into an ambrosial liquid sweetness was only allowed to take place in shrines and sacred places.

In modern Japan, traditional rice malt, called *mizu ame* ("sweet water"), is hard to find. In fact, you may be more likely to find authentic rice malt in an American or European natural foods store than in a modern Japanese supermarket.

One of the few remaining authentic brown rice malt shops is the Uchida Toka Company, in Fukuyama, located in the Hiroshima prefecture. As with other traditional Japanese foods, making brown rice malt is a complex craft requiring a great deal of labor, knowledge, and fine-tuned intuition.

Gunichi Uchida, head of this family-run business, begins the process of making his irresistably sweet yet subtle, thick syrup with crushed and dried organic sprouted barley. The barley is traditionally grown and processed in the mountains around Japan's former capital of Kyoto. Organic barley grains are simply soaked in water until they sprout. They are then dried and crushed, which preserves the delicate enzymes that seeds naturally produce in order to convert their starch into usable sugars for sprouting. Uchida is particularly interested in the enzymes that change the starch into maltose—a di-saccharide sugar used by seeds for sprouting.

First, Uchida flakes brown rice and soaks it overnight. The following morning he steams the flakes for one hour, adding a little water to form a thick porridge called *kayu*. Then, as the porridge is gently stirred, sprouted barley is added.

The delicate enzymes in the sprouted barley are easily destroyed by heat, so Uchida does not let the temperature of his rice porridge go above 158°F. After adding the sprouted barley, Uchida transfers the mixture to a vat, and keeps it at a temperature between 140°–158°F for several hours. During this short time, the carbohydrates, proteins, and fats of the brown rice are broken down into less complex sugars, amino acids, and fatty acids. The longer it is kept, the darker and sweeter the porridge becomes. However, if left for too long, the mixture begins to develop an alcoholic smell and taste. In fact, making rice porridge is one of the steps in the traditional process of making rice wine.

Long before any alcohol develops, Uchida's years of experience tell him it is time to stop the fermentation process by heating the mixture above 158°F. The pasteurized porridge is then transferred to cotton sacks and pressed. As the thick amber liquid drips from the press, it is collected and filtered through cotton cloth.

Finally, the clear-filtered brown rice malt is cooked down for several hours, first by direct cooking and then by steaming. When Uchida feels the malt has reached the perfect thickness, it is filtered one final time and then bottled.

SHOPPING FOR RICE MALT

There are several types of rice syrup available in natural foods, Oriental foods, and grocery stores around the world. Their quality varies from Uchida-style brown rice malt to white rice syrup that is made with enzymes and added sugar. The most common variation of the traditional method is made by substituting laboratory-produced enzymes for the sprouted barley. Another type of rice syrup is made by adding *koji* (cultured rice) to cooked rice and water. Enzymes from the koji act very much like the enzymes found in sprouted grain.

Naturally occurring digestive enzymes, such as those in sprouted barley or koji, are part of a living cell, but by themselves they are not alive. In the laboratory, enzymes are isolated from the rest of the cell and are, therefore, no longer attached to a living system. Producers who use enzymes can control the percentage of maltose and glucose in the final product, and the process is much quicker and more economical.

However, traditional makers of rice malt contend that there is a distinct "qualitative" difference between their product and enzyme-converted rice syrup. "In nature, a cell wouldn't let you use just one or two enzymes," explains rice-syrup authority Jim Allen. "With koji or sprouted barley many enzymes are at work holistically digesting proteins and fats as well as carbohydrates." Gunichi Uchida claims there is a difference in the taste. He feels that with laboratory-produced enzymes you simply cannot get the full range of tastes that you get with sprouted barley.

If you are confused about which rice syrup you are buying, simply read the label. Look for sprouted barley or koji in the ingredients list. Authentic rice or brown rice malt, such as the Uchida products sold under the Mitoku Macrobiotic label, contains whole grain rice, organic sprouted barley, and water. Enzyme-converted rice syrup usually lists rice and water as the only ingredients. Koji-converted rice syrup lists rice, koji, and water. Another grain can be substituted for the rice. For example, the Uchida Toka Company makes the ultimate sweetener (especially for a healing diet) by substituting *hato mugi* (Job's tears) for brown rice in the malt recipe.

Rice malt is a natural food in every sense of the word. The process begins with whole grains and simply lets nature take its course. With gentle warming and occasional stirring, rice malt actually makes itself. No wonder the ancient Japanese considered rice malt to be a gift from the gods. It is!

COOKING WITH RICE MALT

Rice malt has a full, slightly nutty flavor with a hint of butterscotch. Its gentle, balanced sweetness provides the perfect alternative to refined sugar in many snacks and desserts. Rice malt is excellent in salad dressings and dips, as well as in vegetable dishes such as candied yams and pickles.

Rice malt is considerably less sweet than sugar, honey, and maple syrup. To achieve an equivalent sweetness, substitute one and a half cups of rice syrup for one cup of white sugar, three-fourths cup of maple syrup, or one-half cup of honey. When substituting liquid sweeteners for sugar, it is necessary to reduce the total amount of liquid that is called for in the recipe.

If a sweeter taste is desired in the following recipes, or when substituting rice malt for more concentrated sweeteners in other recipes, use a combination of rice malt with honey or maple syrup. A good rule is to initially substitute rice malt for one-half of the maple syrup or honey that is called for in a recipe. Gradually increase the proportion of rice malt until your taste buds are satisfied by desserts that are sweetened with rice malt only.

The texture or thickness of rice malt varies according to the brand and to the temperature at which it is stored. If the malt is too stiff to pour, place the uncovered jar in a saucepan with 2 inches of water and let it simmer a minute or two. When the malt warms up, it will pour easily.

RICE MALT RECIPES

Almond Milk

Use almond milk as a substitute for dairy milk or soymilk in any dessert recipe. Puddings and pie fillings are particularly tasty when almond milk is used.

Water for boiling almonds
1 cup shelled almonds
$\frac{1}{8}$ teaspoon sea salt
1 tablespoon vegetable oil
1 rounded tablespoon rice malt
4 cups cold water

Yield: 1 quart

1. Bring water to a boil in a small pot. Drop in almonds and boil for 10 seconds. Turn off heat and let almonds sit for 2–3 minutes before draining. Transfer almonds to a cold-water bath. When cool enough to handle, remove and discard almond skins.

2. In a blender, combine almonds and remaining ingredients. Blend 1–2 minutes.

3. Strain mixture through cheesecloth, squeezing out all liquid (almond milk) into a quart-sized container.

4. Reserve almond meal in a covered container in the refrigerator. Use meal within 5–6 days in cookies or other pastries.

5. Store almond milk in a covered container in the refrigerator, where it will keep for about 6 days.

Mocha Amazake Pudding

This dairy-free, eggless pudding is delectably sweet with a full, rich flavor.

2 teaspoons carob powder

2 tablespoons grain coffee*

1 cup amazake

1½ cups Almond Milk (page 82),
or ¾ cup each: unflavored soymilk and water

¼ cup rice malt

Pinch sea salt

1½ tablespoons kanten flakes (agar-agar)

1½ tablespoons crushed kuzu

1 teaspoon vanilla

Serves: 4

1. Dissolve carob powder and grain coffee in ¼ cup boiling water.

2. Purée carob mixture, amazake, almond or soymilk, and rice malt in a blender. For a smooth, creamy texture, pour mixture through a fine-mesh strainer to remove any hulls. (Press solids dry and refrigerate in a covered container. Use for cookies or quick breads.)

3. In a medium-sized saucepan, combine amazake mixture and salt. Sprinkle kanten flakes on top, and heat to a simmer over a medium flame without stirring. Simmer 2 minutes, gently stirring until kanten is dissolved.

4. Thoroughly dissolve kuzu in 2 tablespoons cold water and add to pudding while stirring briskly. Simmer 2 minutes more, stirring constantly until pudding thickens.

5. Remove from heat and stir in vanilla. Pour into custard cups or small bowls. Chill until firm before serving (about 2 hours).

*A coffee substitute made primarily from roasted grains.

Blueberry Pie

Nothing satisfies like a homemade fruit pie. This one is extra quick and easy to prepare.

2 pints blueberries, washed and stemmed
³⁄₄ cup rice malt
¹⁄₄ cup granulated tapioca
1 double whole wheat pie crust

Yield: One 9-inch pie

1. Preheat oven to 375°F.

2. In a medium-sized bowl, gently but thoroughly combine blueberries, rice malt, and tapioca. Set aside.

3. Prepare pie crust.

4. Line bottom of a 9-inch pie plate with a layer of crust.

5. Pour fruit mixture into pie shell.

6. Cover with top crust and trim, leaving about ¹⁄₂ inch of crust overhanging the rim of the pie plate. Fold top crust under bottom crust and flute the edges to seal.

7. With a butter knife or paring knife, make several slits in the top crust to allow steam to escape.

8. Bake 50–60 minutes.

9. Cool thoroughly on a wire rack before slicing and serving.

Plum Sorbet

This is a very simple and pretty dessert. Although plums are not as commonly used in frozen desserts as peaches, berries, and citrus fruits, they make an especially lush and creamy sorbet.

6 soft, ripe plums (approximately 1 pound)
$\frac{1}{3}$ cup water
1 $\frac{1}{2}$ teaspoons kanten flakes (agar-agar)
$\frac{2}{3}$–$\frac{3}{4}$ cup rice malt (to taste)
1 teaspoon lemon juice

Yield: 1 pint

1. Halve and pit plums. Combine with $\frac{1}{3}$ cup water in a stainless steel, glass, or enamel-coated saucepan. Bring to a simmer, then cover. Cook gently over medium-low heat, stirring occasionally until tender (10–15 minutes). Remove from heat.

2. With slotted spoon, transfer plums (including skins) to blender or food processor.

3. Sprinkle kanten over remaining cooking liquid and gently simmer 3 minutes, stirring occasionally.

4. Add liquid to blender and purée until smooth.

5. While plums are still hot, mix in rice malt, add lemon juice, and mix well.

6. Pour mixture into a baking pan, casserole dish, or undivided ice tray. Cover with foil or plastic wrap, and freeze until solid (at least 6 hours).

VARIATION

- Plum sorbet is smooth enough to scoop out and eat as is, but for a creamier texture, blend it again (at least one hour and up to a day before serving). Scrape frozen mixture with a fork until it resembles finely crushed ice. Spoon half of mixture into a chilled food-processor bowl or blender and purée until light and smooth but not thawed. Process the other half. Place blended sorbet in a pint container, cover, and freeze until firm (1–3 hours).

Candied Yams

Brighten up your winter days with this delectable side dish. A real treat!

3 medium yams,
peeled and cut into $\frac{1}{4}$-inch-thick rounds or diagonal slices
3 tablespoons rice malt
$\frac{1}{2}$ teaspoon sesame or canola oil
1 teaspoon finely grated lemon peel

Serves: 6

1. Preheat oven to 325°F.

2. Steam yams until just tender, then arrange in a single layer on a lightly oiled baking sheet.

3. Combine remaining ingredients and spread a thin layer of syrup mixture over each yam slice. Bake 5 minutes.

4. Arrange on a platter and serve.

7

TOASTED SESAME OIL
Cooking Oil Supreme

The old castle town of Aizu lies deep in the mountains several hours north of Tokyo. During the last century, Aizu was the scene of fierce fighting as the last of the samurai *daimyos* resisted Imperial forces in an attempt to keep their power. Today Aizu is a cultural center known for the quality of its lacquerware and other fine crafts of old Japan. Here, in this historic town, is the Hiraide family sesame-oil shop, one of the last authentic oil pressers.

Sesame oil is a supreme cooking oil; its rich flavor has made it an essential ingredient in the finest Japanese cuisine. What's more, sesame oil is one of the world's purest and healthiest cooking oils. It is high in linoleic acid, one of the three essential fatty acids (EFAs) our bodies cannot produce. Essential fatty acids are necessary for normal growth and for healthy blood, arteries, and nerves. They keep the skin and other tissues youthful and healthy by preventing dryness and scaliness. Recent scientific research has shown that EFAs also play an important role in regulating blood pressure, cholesterol metabolism, and the flow of biochemicals across cell membranes.

PRESERVING A TRADITIONAL PROCESS

Tama shibori or "simple pressing" is the traditional process used at the Hiraide shop. Without high temperatures or chemicals, this centuries-old method produces sesame oil with a fresh nutty taste and aroma, while retaining most of the oil's original healthful qualities.

The Hiraide family begins by selecting golden sesame seeds, the very best available. The seeds are slowly toasted in a unique wood-fired toasting machine. According to Kichisaburo Hiraide, the fifth generation head of the family shop, wood toasting heats the seeds from the inside out. In contrast, says Hiraide, "electric toasting heats from the outside in, which gives typical toasted sesame oil a subtle harshness not found in wood-fired oils."

Next, the toasted seeds are crushed by simple rollers and then lightly steamed for a few minutes. Steaming heats and moistens the seeds, which allows the oil to flow more freely.

The steamed sesame meal is placed in a wooden pressing tub that is lined with two types of filters, one made of paper and the other made of human hair. (The few remaining Japanese oil makers who still use filters made from human hair claim it gives their oil its characteristic "soft texture.") The tub of warm sesame meal is then pressed.

With gentle pressure, the crushed sesame seeds easily release their rich, golden oil, which passes through the filter and drips from the bottom of the tub. This first pressing is called *ichiban shibori*; its warm, nutty aroma fills the old workshop. Filtered once more, this time through hand-made Japanese paper, the oil is bottled immediately without the use of preservatives.

When stored at room temperature and exposed to air and light, most natural vegetable oils gradually turn rancid. Fortunately, a minute amount of sesamol—a natural by-product of sesame seeds—protects sesame oil from oxidation. This is why sesame oil, of all the edible oils, is the least subject to rancidity and loss of flavor over time.

The simple, but labor-intense methods used by the Hiraide family for over 150 years may seem impractical by modern manufacturing standards. Kichisaburo Hiraide and his son Yuichi produce a modest thirty quarts of oil for a full day's work. In contrast, large oil companies produce thousands of gallons a day with little effort.

However, the high-speed industrial oil-extraction process strips oil of its flavor, aroma, natural color, and nutritional value. To insure that every last drop of oil is extracted from sesame seeds, commercial manufacturers add hexane—a petroleum-based solvent—to crushed seeds during pressing. The hexane-extracted oil is then neutralized with sodium hydroxide and deodorized by heating to 400°F.

Comparing Hiraide's oil with the typical toasted sesame oil found in Oriental foods stores, which is usually made using the industrial extraction process, the significance of simple pressing becomes obvious. The commercial product is dark, overpowering, and has a harsh aroma. By contrast, the Hiraide product, available in the United States under the Mitoku Macrobiotic label, is light in color and smells and tastes like freshly toasted sesame seeds; it has a distinctive feel, which has been described as "soft and silky."

Hiraide toasted sesame oil is more than a delicious, healthful food. In a sense, it is one of Aizu's cultural treasures, a vestige of old Japan.

COOKING WITH TOASTED SESAME OIL

The delightfully nutty flavor and aroma of toasted sesame oil is a distinctive characteristic of Oriental cooking. Like other oils, toasted sesame oil seals in nutrients and prevents burning when sautéeing, baking, and pan-frying, but its appetizing fragrance and rich taste make this oil most highly prized as a seasoning.

Use a small amount of toasted sesame oil in marinades, vinaigrettes, sauces, and dressings. Toasted sesame oil will enhance the flavor of fried noodles and sautéed or stir-fried dishes. Add about 10 percent toasted sesame oil to the oil used for tempura or deep-frying. This will give the cooking oil a rich, background flavor. In sautéeing, most natural toasted sesame oils may overpower some mild-flavored vegetables if used alone, but it is delicious when used in combination with another vegetable oil, such as light sesame or canola.

The easiest way to take advantage of sesame oil's rich flavor is in braised vegetable dishes. Simply sauté a few thin slices of ginger in two or three teaspoons of toasted sesame oil. To this, add vegetables such as broccoli, kale, or cabbage and a pinch of salt. Sauté briefly, then add a little water. Cover and simmer until the vegetables are tender.

TOASTED SESAME OIL RECIPES

Braised Gingered Broccoli

Chinese cooks have long known that the combination of toasted sesame oil and ginger can elevate the simplest dishes into offerings fit for your most honored guests. Any number of vegetables can be substituted for the broccoli in this recipe. Sliced cabbage, kale, carrots, or green beans are excellent choices.

2 teaspoons toasted sesame oil

4–5 thin slices peeled fresh ginger root

1 bunch broccoli

Pinch sea salt

1 teaspoon natural soy sauce

$1\frac{1}{2}$–2 teaspoons lemon juice (optional)

Serves: 4–5

1. In a large skillet or saucepan, heat oil and sauté ginger over medium-low heat for 1 minute.

2. Cut broccoli into bite-sized florets, and peel and slice stems on the diagonal. Add broccoli and salt to the skillet, sauté a minute more, then add water to cover the bottom of pan. Cover and steam until broccoli is just tender-crisp and still bright green (about 5 minutes).

3. Uncover broccoli, sprinkle with soy sauce and, if desired, lemon juice. Toss and serve.

Shrimp Japonais

Here's a main course that is special enough to serve guests yet quick and easy to prepare. Shrimp Japonais is perfect when served with a simple clear soup, blanched broccoli or green beans, and a bowl of rice.

1 pound large or jumbo shrimp
2 ½ tablespoons toasted sesame oil
1 large onion, halved and thinly sliced lengthwise
3 ½ cups sliced mushrooms
2 cloves garlic, finely minced
2 tablespoons sake or dry white wine
3 scallions, thinly sliced on the diagonal

MARINADE
3 tablespoons mellow white miso
3 tablespoons mirin
2 tablespoons sake or dry white wine
1 teaspoon shoyu
2 teaspoons fresh ginger juice

Serves: 4

1. Peel and devein shrimp, leaving on the tails.

2. Combine marinade ingredients in a small bowl and mix well.

3. Add shrimp, toss to coat well, and marinate 45 minutes to an hour, stirring occasionally.

4. Heat oil in a wok or skillet over medium-high heat. Shake excess marinade off shrimp and sauté them until just pink (2 minutes). Remove shrimp and set aside.

5. If necessary, add another teaspoon of oil to moisten the pan. Sauté onion until tender, stirring quickly and constantly to prevent burning. Next, add mushrooms and garlic, and sauté until fragrant (2–3 minutes).

6. Add sake or wine and 1 tablespoon of marinade and toss. Add scallions and sauté until just wilted but still bright green (about 30 seconds). Add shrimp and toss.

7. Remove from pan and serve immediately.

Fancy Scrambled Tofu

This delicious and eye-appealing dish is from our friend Debbie Athos, an experienced macrobiotic cooking instructor. She served us this fancy version of scrambled tofu as the centerpiece of a Sunday brunch. If you are in a hurry, she suggests eliminating the corn, peppers, and scallion. Serve with grits and toast.

1 tablespoon sesame oil
1 onion, finely diced
$\frac{1}{2}$ red bell pepper, seeded and diced
2 ears cooked corn
2 scallions, thinly sliced on the diagonal
1 pound fresh tofu
1–1 $\frac{1}{2}$ tablespoons shoyu (to taste)
Chopped parsley for garnish
Powdered kelp or toasted black sesame seeds (optional)

Serves: 4

1. Heat oil in a cast iron or other heavy skillet over medium-high heat. Add onion and sauté 3 minutes.

2. Add red pepper to skillet and sauté 2 minutes.

3. With a sharp knife, cut kernels from corn cobs. Add corn and scallions to skillet, and sauté 1 minute.

4. With your hands, crumble tofu into skillet, add shoyu to taste, and "scramble" tofu for 5 minutes.

5. Garnish with parsley and, if desired, kelp or black sesame seeds. Serve hot.

Seitan Fried Rice

Delicious and satisfying, yet quick and easy to prepare, this dish is a good way to use leftover cooked rice. Seitan Fried Rice goes well when accompanied by bean soup and a side dish of steamed greens.

1 tablespoon toasted sesame oil
2 cloves garlic, finely minced (optional)
1 small carrot, cut into matchsticks
Pinch sea salt
1 tablespoon mirin (optional)
4 scallions, sliced on the diagonal in $\frac{1}{4}$-inch lengths
1 teaspoon shoyu or tamari
$\frac{1}{2}$ cup thin seitan strips
$\frac{1}{2}$-inch piece fresh ginger, peeled and finely minced
2 cups cooked rice
Minced scallion or parsley for garnish

Serves: 2

1. Heat oil in a skillet over medium heat, add garlic (if using), and sauté 1 minute. Be careful not to brown garlic.

2. Add carrots, salt, and mirin (or 1 tablespoon water) and sauté briefly.

3. Add scallions and sauté 3–5 minutes (carrots should still be a little crunchy but not raw tasting).

4. Lower heat and add soy sauce, seitan, and ginger. Sauté briefly.

5. Add rice, breaking up any clumps with side of a wooden spoon. Mix thoroughly, cover, and cook 1–2 minutes more.

6. Serve hot with garnish of minced scallion or parsley.

8

SHIITAKE
Miracle Mushrooms

Shiitake, Japanese forest mushrooms, are one of the Orient's most exotic and delicious foods. Shiitake's delicate, yet wild, woodsy taste adds a gourmet flair to almost any dish. Moreover, all eight amino acids are present in a ratio similar to the "ideal" protein for human nutrition. Shiitake are rich in the amino acids leucine and lysine, which are deficient in many grains. Shiitake are also a good source of B vitamins, including the ever-elusive B_{12}. (Vitamin B_{12} is synthesized solely by bacteria and fungi, and is not available from vegetables.) It is, however, shiitake's medicinal possibilities that are getting worldwide attention. In the last two decades, scientists have isolated substances from shiitake that may play a role in the cure and prevention of modern civilization's dreaded illnesses: heart disease, cancer, and AIDS.

Biologists consider shiitake and other mushrooms to be fungi, a group of primitive plants. Since they have no green pigments (chlorophyll), they cannot make food from sunlight as other plants, but must live by eating plants or animals.

Shiitake's favorite food is dead hardwood trees. The word "shii" is derived from the shii tree *(Quercus cuspidata)*, an oak of central and southern Japan upon which shiitake most often grow. "Take" means mushroom in Japanese (it is repetitious to say "shiitake mushroom").

The part of shiitake that we eat, the fleshy cap, is actually a primitive reproductive structure. You may have noticed a gray or beige powder on the undersurface of opened mushrooms. These are billions of microscopic spores. Like sperm and eggs (ova) of animals, the spores are sex cells. Each spore carries half the genetic information of their parent mushroom. Mushroom spores move about the forest with the help of wind and rain. When two compatible spores get together, they fuse their cytoplasm and genetic material and, if food is available, grow into a new mushroom. This new plant is a white filimentous subterranean growth called a *mycelium*. In the case of shiitake, mycelium grows inside the log, using its powerful enzymes to change wood into food. After a period of time, environmental stresses such as food depletion or temperature and humidity changes cause the mycelium to form a reproductive structure—the mushroom—and the cycle is complete.

GROWING SHIITAKE

Left to their own devices, shiitake would probably rather reproduce by the sexual cycle outlined above. However, to insure crop quality and consistency, shiitake growers inoculate their logs with the mushroom mycelium rather than spores. The so-called vegetative (asexual) method begins by growing shiitake mycelium on wood chips, paper disks, or "enriched" sawdust. Shiitake cultivators then insert these "spawn" into holes or cuts made in hardwood logs.

In early fall, as trees shed their leaves in preparation for a dormant winter, the carbohydrate level in the tree trunk rises, making an ideal food for shiitake growth. When about 10 percent of the leaves have fallen, shiitake growers fell trees and cut them into three-foot logs. Next, about twenty to twenty-five evenly spaced holes are drilled into each log. Then wood chips (plug spawn) are hammered into the holes. When sawdust spawn are used, they are placed in holes using a special transfer tool. In both cases, the holes are sealed with hot wax.

After the logs are inoculated, they are carried into a pine forest and placed in a spot where there is an ideal balance of sunlight and shade. Usually, by the following fall, the shiitake mycelium has completely penetrated the logs, and, with seasonal temperature changes, mushrooms begin to push through the bark.

From just one inoculation, logs can be expected to produce crops of shiitake every fall and spring for three to five years, until the logs are completely decayed. The variety of shiitake called *donko*, are superior in both flavor and medicinal qualities to the variety called *koshin*. In their natural effort at self-preservation, donko shiitake produce a thick cap with strong viable spores to protect against harsh environmental conditions.

The harvesting time of shiitake is very important. If the mushroom is left on the log too long, it will completely open and shed its spores, producing a mushroom that is thin, flat, dark, and lacking in vitality. According to Fusataro Taniguchi, the grower of Mitoku Macrobiotic premium sun-dried shiitake, donko shiitake (picked at the right time) should not be more than 70 percent open and should have thick, fleshy, slightly rounded caps. These cost more but are prized for their excellent flavor and healthfulness.

The "natural log" method of growing shiitake is still practiced by most of the Orient's shiitake farmers. However, in the West, where shiitake farming is relatively new, the high-tech method of growing shiitake indoors under controlled conditions on "synthetic sawdust logs" (actually sawdust blocks) is used by approximately 80 percent of the large commercial growers.

The method of growing shiitake on sawdust logs is a direct outcome of the biotechnical revolution that has taken place since World War II. Drawing on the latest technology, exotic mushroom cultivators mix various nutrients into sawdust, which is then formed into a block, sterilized, and inoculated with shiitake mycelium. The blocks are then placed in semi-sterile growing rooms under "ideal conditions" to maximize mushroom growth.

CULTIVATION CONTROVERSY

The controversy over which method of cultivation produces the most delicious and nutritious mushroom is a heated debate in the exclusive world of exotic mushrooms. Taniguchi and other traditional shiitake growers feel that shiitake grown on synthetic sawdust logs look and taste inferior to their natural log-grown mushrooms. In addition, they believe that the fungicides used to control pests in the semi-sterile growing rooms pose a health threat to consumers and workers. The Organic Crop Improvement Association (OCIA), an internationally recognized organic certification group, does not consider shiitake grown on sawdust logs organic. According to OCIA literature, only natural trees (not synthetic compost logs) can be used in the cultivation of exotic mushrooms. The OCIA also states that the use of any pesticide for partial or total indoor cultivation is prohibited.

However, such criticism about sawdust-grown shiitake is hotly contested. Some growers who use sawdust logs boast that the rapid-cycle system, using nutrient-enriched sawdust logs and no fungicides, can produce excellent shiitake in just thirty-five days. What's more, they claim that their shiitake look and taste as good or better than log-grown shiitake.

To get a more balanced point of view about the natural-versus-synthetic log controversy, we interviewed Professor Paul Wuest, author and professor of Plant Pathology at Pennsylvania State University. "Shiitake grown on sawdust under ideal conditions can be as good as log grown," said Wuest. He also said that larger commercial growers are usually forced to use some fungicides to keep other molds from growing on the sawdust logs.

Since most dried shiitake are grown outdoors on logs, there is a better chance of avoiding fungicides by purchasing dried shiitake, particularly those sold in natural foods stores. Japanese natural foods exporters, such as Mitoku, specify that their shiitake are not sprayed with fungicides. Moreover, Mitoku grower Fusataro Taniguchi feels that shiitake grown outdoors, subject to the rigors of the natural environment, have more concentrated medicinal properties and flavor.

MEDICINAL QUALITIES OF SHIITAKE

The person most responsible for stimulating the current medicinal interest in shiitake was Japan's Kisaku Mori, Ph.D. In 1936, Dr. Mori established the Institute of Mushroom Research in Tokyo. Until his death in 1977, Dr. Mori worked with scientists from around the world to document the medicinal effects of shiitake. Using analytical techniques, Mori found shiitake high in many enzymes and vitamins that were not usually found in plants. His findings, published in *Mushrooms as Health Foods*, were extensive. Working for years with human subjects, he discovered that shiitake was effective in treating a long list of ailments including high cholesterol, gallstones, hyperacidity, stomach ulcers, diabetes, vitamin deficiency, anemia, and even the common cold.

Mori's work gained notoriety, particularly in Japanese medicinal circles, and, beginning in the 1960s, scientists launched an extensive search to uncover the secret of shiitake's legendary healing powers. Their studies—about one hundred in all—have focused on shiitake's ability to rapidly lower serum cholesterol, as well as this mushroom's potent antitumor, antiviral, and antibiotic properties.

High levels of cholesterol in the blood have been linked to serious diseases such as arteriosclerosis and strokes, so investigators were excited in 1966 when they isolated a substance from shiitake that dramatically lowered blood cholesterol. This substance, now called *eritadenine*, was given to rats on a high-cholesterol diet. In just a few days, as reported in *The Journal of Nutrition*, the blood cholesterol level of the rats dropped 25 to 45 percent. Eritadenine has been associated with the water-soluble fiber of shiitake, but its action is even stronger when the whole mushroom is consumed. Studies with humans have shown that only three ounces of shiitake (5–6 mushrooms) a day can lower cholesterol 12 percent in a week.

"Many of the human diseases currently increasing throughout the world have no specific cures," notes mycologist John Donoghue, co-author of *Shiitake Growers Handbook.* "Immune-system failure or dysfunction is a common element in cancer, viruses, and immune-deficiency diseases," says Donoghue. He and other scientists around the world contend that there is increasing evidence that the health-promoting compounds found in medicinal and edible fungi, including shiitake, stimulate the immune system.

Scientists now believe that a polysaccharide called *lentinan* and virus-like particles found in shiitake trigger the increased production of various serum factors associated with immunity and inflammation. These so-called *lymphokines,* such as interferon and interleukin, stimulate the defense system, spurring the proliferation of phagocytes, including macrophages and other immune fighters that attack cancer cells, bacteria, and viruses.

The most dramatic experiment demonstrating shiitake's antitumor effect was performed on animals. At the National Cancer Research Center in Tokyo, mice suffering from sarcoma, a type of virally-induced cancer, were treated with small doses of shiitake extract over short periods of time. In 1970, the results, published in the United States journal *Cancer Research,* showed that six out of ten mice had complete tumor regression. At slightly higher concentrations, shiitake was 100 percent effective—all mice showed tumor regression.

Similar studies have shown that shiitake extract helps prevent transplanted tumors from taking hold, and "excellent results" were obtained by Japanese scientists in a four-year follow-up study of patients with advanced and recurrent stomach and colon cancer. Shiitake extract is even being tested for use with modern chemotherapy drugs to lessen their toxic effects on healthy tissue and the immune system.

The most recent development in shiitake medical research involves the use of shiitake extract to inhibit the reproduction of human immunodeficiency virus (HIV) in tissue culture. Researchers working at Japan's Yamaguchi University School of Medicine have reported that shiitake extract has a "protective effect" that inhibits the usual cell-destroying effects of the HIV virus. Researchers have noted that substances such as shiitake, which both enhance the immune response and have antiviral effects, should be further evaluated for the treatment of AIDS.

In addition to fighting cancer, inhibiting the growth of viruses, and lowering cholesterol, shiitake have potent antibiotic effects against other organisms. A substance called *cortinelin,* a broad-spectrum antibacterial agent, which has been isolated from shiitake, kills a wide range of pathogenic bacteria. A sulfide compound extracted from shiitake has been found to have an effect against the fungus that causes ringworm and other skin diseases.

A Mushroom A Day...

Long before they were cultivated, wild shiitake were used as a potent medicine by ancient Oriental herbologists. As culture developed and healing became more specialized, herbalists began concentrating the shiitake's active ingredients by boiling or slow-cooking the mushrooms to make medicinal teas and pastes. These special preparations have a long history in Oriental folklore for the treatment of tumors, flu, heart disease, high blood pressure, obesity, and problems related to sexual dysfunction and aging.

COOKING WITH SHIITAKE

Shiitake or other healing mushrooms should be enjoyed as part of a daily diet. Dr. Mori recommended four shiitake a day for the maintenance of health. However, when using shiitake as part of a therapeutic regimen, much larger doses are usually recommended.

The temperatures of cooking do not seem to destroy shiitake's healing qualities. In addition, cooking greatly enhances the mushroom's flavor. You can cook fresh shiitake in all the ways you are used to enjoying other mushrooms—in soups, stews, sauces, and gravies. Shiitake are a flavorful addition to fried rice, noodles, and stir-fried dishes. They are particularly delicious in tempura or when baked with a seasoning of shoyu, mirin, and fresh ginger. For a special treat, brush shiitake caps with olive oil and grill three to four minutes.

To clean fresh shiitake, simply wipe them with a damp cloth or soft brush. Fresh shiitake can also be rinsed under cold water and patted dry, but be careful not to soak them or they will become soggy.

Dried shiitake are readily available in Oriental markets and natural foods stores and are becoming more popular in supermarkets. Though the texture of reconstituted dried shiitake is not as tender as that of the fresh mushrooms, shiitake's exquisite flavor is even more concentrated with drying. To reconstitute, submerge the dried shiitake in water for at least one or two hours, preferably overnight. After soaking, cut off and discard the tough stems and slice the caps. The soaking water makes a wonderful rich stock for soups, stews, sauces, and gravies. Used with their soaking water and other ingredients, such as carrots and greens, shiitake are a superb addition to miso soup.

Regardless of the type of food you enjoy, shiitake will add rich flavor and vitality to your diet. Following are several of our family's favorite shiitake recipes.

SHIITAKE RECIPES

Dashi
(All-Purpose Soup Stock)

This simple stock is great for soups (especially veggie or miso); stews; sauces and gravies; noodle broths; and dips for tempura, fried mochi, and fried tofu. Dashi will keep for one week in the refrigerator. It can be frozen in a well-sealed container and kept indefinitely.

6-inch-piece kombu
3 dried shiitake
7 cups spring water

Yield: Approximately 6 cups

1. In a pot, soak kombu and shiitake in water 15 minutes. Remove shiitake, cut off and discard stems, and thinly slice caps.

2. Return mushroom caps to water, and heat over medium flame. Remove kombu just before water boils.

3. Reduce heat and simmer 5 minutes before removing shiitake from finished broth.

4. Reserve kombu and shiitake for another use.

Hot and Spicy Chinese Noodle Soup

Ginger and chili-flavored sesame oil give this dish an authentic Oriental flavor.

6 cups water
5 dried shiitake
2 slices peeled fresh ginger root
1 teaspoon sea salt
1/2 cup thinly sliced carrots
1/3 cup diced red bell pepper or thinly sliced celery
1/2 package (2 1/2 ounces) clear noodles (bifun or saifun)
12 snow peas, each trimmed and diagonally cut into 2–3 pieces
2 teaspoons natural soy sauce
1/4 teaspoon chili-flavored sesame oil*

Serves: 6

1. In a pot, submerge shiitake in water and soak 2 hours or longer. Remove shiitake, cut off and discard stems, and thinly slice caps. Return caps to soaking water.

2. Add ginger to the shiitake stock and gently simmer 10 minutes. Remove and discard ginger.

3. Add salt, carrots, and bell pepper or celery, and simmer 10 minutes.

4. While soup is simmering, boil noodles in another pot for 5–6 minutes. Rinse cooked noodles under cold running water, drain well, and chop into 2-inch lengths. Divide noodles among individual serving bowls.

5. To the simmering pot, add snow peas and soy sauce and simmer a minute more. Add chili-flavored sesame oil and remove from heat.

6. Ladle hot soup over noodles and serve.

---

*Chili-flavored sesame oil is available in most well-stocked natural foods stores, Asian food stores, and some specialty shops and supermarkets.

Shiitake Gravy

This flavorful gravy will enhance all your favorite grain dishes.

2 dried shiitake

2 cups water

1 $\frac{1}{2}$ tablespoons extra virgin olive oil

1 small onion, diced

2 cloves garlic, finely minced

3 tablespoons unbleached white flour

$\frac{1}{4}$ teaspoon sea salt

$\frac{1}{2}$ teaspoon natural soy sauce

$\frac{1}{2}$ teaspoon dried thyme

1 tablespoon mirin or white wine

Yield: 1 $\frac{1}{2}$ cups

1. In a bowl, submerge shiitake in water and soak 2 hours or longer. Remove shiitake, cut off and discard stems, and thinly slice or chop caps.

2. Heat oil in a medium-sized skillet. Add shiitake, onion, and garlic. Sauté over medium-low heat until onion is translucent.

3. Lower heat, sprinkle flour over vegetables, and stir constantly for 2–3 minutes.

4. Slowly add soaking water while stirring briskly to prevent the flour from lumping. Stir frequently until gravy begins to simmer and thicken.

5. Add salt, soy sauce, thyme, and mirin or wine. Simmer gently, uncovered, for about 15 minutes, stirring occasionally.* Keep warm until ready to serve.

---

*If gravy is too thick, add a little more stock or water. If too thin, cook down to desired consistency or slowly stir in 1–2 teaspoons crushed kuzu or arrowroot that has been dissolved in an equal amount of cold water. Stir until gravy thickens.

Shiitake Consommé

Consommés, or clear soups, are simple and elegant. Though they can be served anytime, their lightness makes them especially appealing in warm weather or as an accompaniment to large, festive meals.

3 dried shiitake

7 cups water

6-inch-piece kombu

1 ½ tablespoons tamari or shoyu (or slightly more to taste)

1–1 ½ tablespoons mirin

½ teaspoon sea salt

20–30 carrot slices*

Small handful watercress sprigs, cut into 2–3 pieces
(parboiled spinach or other tender greens can be substituted)

Peeled, finely grated ginger root (approximately 1 pinch per serving)

Serves: 6

1. In a medium-sized pot, submerge shiitake in water and soak at least 2 hours.

2. Add kombu and bring to a simmer over medium heat. Remove kombu as soon as water begins to simmer, and reserve it for another use. Continue to simmer shiitake 5–10 minutes. Remove the mushrooms, cut off and discard stems, and thinly slice caps. Return shiitake to stock.

3. Add soy sauce, mirin, and salt to the stock and bring just to a simmer. If not using immediately, remove from heat and reheat just before serving.

4. In a separate pot, parboil carrot slices until just tender.

5. Remove sliced shiitake from broth and divide among six soup bowls.

6. Divide and arrange carrots, raw watercress or parboiled greens, and ginger in soup bowls. Cover with piping hot broth and serve immediately.

---

*For a creative touch, carrot slices can be shaped into flowers by scalloping the edges.

Braised Kale and Shiitake

Mediterranean and Japanese influences blend perfectly in this delectable fall or winter side dish.

3 dried shiitake
Water for soaking shiitake
1 tablespoon extra virgin olive oil
3 cloves garlic, finely minced
1 bunch kale, chopped
2 pinches sea salt
Shoyu or tamari (to taste)

Serves: 4

1. Submerge shiitake in bowl of lukewarm water and soak 2 hours or longer. Remove mushrooms, cut off and discard stems, and thinly slice caps. Reserve soaking water.

2. Heat oil in a large skillet over medium-low heat. Add garlic and shiitake and sauté briefly (be careful not to let the garlic brown, which causes bitterness). Toss in pinch of salt.

3. Add kale and sauté 1–2 minutes. Add another pinch of salt, toss, and add shiitake soaking water (or fresh water) to cover bottom of pan. Cover and cook until greens are just tender.

4. Add light sprinkle of shoyu or tamari. Toss and serve.

9

SOY SAUCE
King of Condiments

The world's love affair with Japanese soy sauce may have begun with Dutch traders who were stationed in Nagasaki during the seventeenth century. Those early middlemen sent barrels of this liquid treasure back to Europe, some of which ended up in the royal kitchens of Louis XV of France (1645–1715). It was rumored around the court that the king's secret ingredient came from the other side of the globe, where it had been fermented for almost two years in three-meter-tall wooden casks. Since that time, Japanese soy sauce, with its rich, fermented fragrance and salty, sweet, slightly tart flavor, has secured an international reputation as a versatile and delicious seasoning.

Although Westerners now indiscriminately sprinkle soy sauce on everything from beef to popcorn, experienced cooks use it with discretion to enhance the subtle, natural flavors of foods. But beware: the dark, thick seasoning enjoyed by yesterday's European aristocrats is very different from most of the soy sauce sold in supermarkets today. Almost half of the 60 million dollars Americans spend annually on soy sauce is for a product containing soy extract, ethyl alcohol, sugar, salt, food coloring, and preservatives. Not fermented, this product is the result of a one-day chemical process. Nearly all of the remaining soy sauce sold in the United States is made from chemically processed soy meal and contains sodium benzoate as a preservative. High-tech, accelerated methods and temperature-controlled fermentation are used in the manufacturing of this product.

If you want to experience the true flavor of traditional Japanese soy sauce, usually called *shoyu* or *tamari*, read labels carefully. Traditional shoyu is made with water, whole soybeans, wheat, and sea salt; contains no preservatives (naturally occurring alcohol from wheat fermentation acts as a preservative); and is unhurriedly aged in wooden casks at natural temperatures for eighteen months to two years. Tamari is made by a similar process, but it contains no wheat. Small amounts of alcohol or rice wine may be added as a natural preservative. Less than 1 percent of all Japanese soy sauce is made using traditional ingredients and methods.

William Shurtleff, a scholar of Japanese foods and co-author of *The Book of Miso*, points to *miso tamari* as the forerunner of modern soy sauce. Miso tamari is the dark, thick liquid that accumulates in fermenting miso (soybean paste). By the twelfth century, brewers were preparing miso tamari from a special type of miso and were selling it commercially. However, this tamari was more closely related to present-day wheat-free tamari than to today's typical Japanese shoyu.

Around the fifteenth century, the word shoyu appeared in a Japanese dictionary. At first, shoyu was a tamari-like product with roasted barley added. By the eighteenth century, brewers had discovered that the addition of wheat gave the tamari a richer flavor and aroma. Further experimentation in the eighteenth and nineteenth centuries led to the traditional recipe of 50 percent wheat and 50 percent soybeans (or soy meal) now adhered to by both high-tech and traditional manufacturers. Today, the Japanese term shoyu, when used by Westerners, usually refers to fermented soy sauce with wheat, particularly the traditional product. Tamari usually refers to the wheat-free soy sauce, which is still made in small quantities in central Japan.

SHOYU

In the natural foods industry the name Johsen is synonymous with shoyu (soy sauce made with wheat). In fact, many of the world's best-selling natural food brands are actually Johsen bottled under other distributors' labels. But even in Japan, where top-quality shoyu must meet the highest standards, Johsen shoyu is considered the best. In 1988, Johsen shoyu received the Japanese Ministry of Agriculture's first place award for "the highest quality soy sauce in Japan." It was selected from over 2,000 entries by a panel of the world's foremost shoyu experts.

During a two-week visit several years ago, we were able to observe how Johsen traditional shoyu is made and to learn firsthand the way Sendai Shoyu and Miso Company of Sendai, Japan assumed an important role in the world's natural foods movement.

THE JOHSEN PROCESS

The Johsen process of making shoyu begins with the roasting and cracking of whole winter wheat and the steaming of whole soybeans. These ingredients are then mixed together in approximately equal parts and inoculated with spores of *Aspergillus* mold. After a three-day incubation period in a warm, humid room, the wheat and soybeans are covered with a fragrant, fluffy mold mycelium that is high in natural enzymes. Now called *koji*, the mixture is added to a brine solution of water, sea salt, and nigari (the mineral residue that remains after sodium chloride is extracted from sea water). In temperate climates, the thick mixture of koji and brine, called *moromi*, is placed in seasoned cedar casks to ferment for about eighteen months (or at least two full summers).

During the long aging process, enzymes from the koji and the naturally occurring yeasts and bacteria slowly break down the complex carbohydrates, proteins, and oils of the wheat and soybeans into sweet sugars, aromatic alcohol, and flavorful amino and fatty acids. The mature fermented moromi is then placed in cotton sacks and pressed under great force to extract its dark liquid, a mixture of shoyu and crude soy oil. The oil, which rises to the surface, is removed. Now, the shoyu is ready for settling, low-temperature pasteurization, and bottling. The entire process takes about twenty-four months.

AN IMPRESSIVE TOUR

From the outside, Sendai Shoyu and Miso Company's towering soybean silos are not unlike those of other modern Japanese soy-sauce factories. However, as company brewmaster Ko Haga began our tour, the emphasis on quality and detail—the hallmarks of the company—was immediately apparent. First, we noticed two women carefully inspecting whole soybeans and picking out imperfect ones as the beans passed before them on a conveyor belt. Next, we were asked to remove our shoes and don special slippers before entering the immaculate manufacturing area.

Inside the kura, the fermenting shoyu moromi is stirred.

As the brewmaster walked us through the traditional shoyu process, we looked forward with anticipation to seeing the *kura*, the fermentation warehouse. We were not disappointed. We entered an atmosphere filled with the heady aroma of yeast and sweet alcohol. An elderly man walked on an elevated platform between rows of cedar casks seven feet wide and ten feet deep, gently stirring each batch of thick, fermenting moromi with a long wooden pole. We returned to the dark kura many times during our busy two-week visit. It was a perfect place to relax and feel the spirit of old Japan.

THE STRUGGLE TO PRESERVE NATURAL SHOYU

In the formal setting of his small office in the Sendai Shoyu and Miso Company, seventy-nine-year-old Jubei Sasaki, eighth-generation company president and outspoken natural foods advocate, told us of his family's long struggle to keep traditional shoyu alive. According to Sasaki, during the American occupation of his country after World War II, severe shortages of raw materials prompted many manufacturers to experiment with faster, less expensive ways of making shoyu.

At first, unfermented soy sauce was made using Hydrolyzed Vegetable Protein (HVP), but the taste was so objectionable to most Japanese that the experiment was discontinued. Next, the shoyu industry, aided by developments in microbiology and food-processing technology, turned to speeding up the expensive and lengthy traditional process. Sasaki recalled that, at first, the new innovations seemed to offer a better product at a lower price. Less expensive, defatted soy meal—which replaced costly whole soybeans—fermented faster because it contained less fat (soy oil), which is difficult for microorganisms to break down. The introduction of temperature controls further accelerated fermentation, since aging shoyu no longer had to lay dormant during the colder months. By using temperature controls and defatted soy meal, high-tech shoyu producers increased their annual yields 300 to 400 percent. The final break with tradition came more recently. The hand-crafted cedar casks, which are held together with braided bamboo hoops, were replaced by concrete, stainless steel, and plastic tanks, which can be cleaned and maintained with less effort.

Sasaki admitted that the chemical analysis of high-tech shoyu compares favorably with the traditional product. Although it does not have the rich taste and aroma of traditionally made shoyu (because it contains less alcohol and glutamic acid), the high-tech product does have more nitrogen, which may indicate a more efficient utilization of raw materials. The technologists were pleased, but Sasaki and other traditionalists were skeptical. Could hexane-treated soy meal replace whole soybeans? Sasaki also suspected that the vigorous fermentation process (which takes place during the summer), coupled with the subtle winter activity, influenced the developing moromi. Sasaki believed the traditional method slowly transformed and mellowed the mixture in a way that could not be duplicated by artificial temperature controls.

Sasaki recalled, however, that "It was the substitution of synthetic tanks for wooden casks that caused the greatest concern." Ironically, Sasaki explained, even today, some Japanese high-tech shoyu manufacturers still use old cedar casks when possible. Their reasoning, which has never been scientifically tested and is often disputed by other high-tech shoyu producers, is that seasoned wooden casks contribute subtleties of flavor and distinctive character to fermented foods. After years of use, the cracks and crevices of the wood are home to the myriad microorganisms that reinoculate new batches of shoyu and facilitate the fermentation process. Wooden-cask advocates claim that the influence of these organisms, along with the flavor imparted by the natural oils in the cedar, add to the deep, rich taste and unique character of wood-fermented foods.

Fortunately for shoyu connoisseurs and the natural foods industry, the Sasaki family did not completely give in to post-war economic pressures. Although Sendai Shoyu and Miso Company started making high-tech shoyu in 1950, Sasaki insisted that his company also continue to make traditional shoyu. For many years there were few buyers of the more expensive shoyus that were made using the traditional Johsen process, and Sasaki was often forced to sell his product at a loss. At times, it seemed his pet project was a financial disaster. However, in 1970 he received a phone call from Akiyoshi Kazama, president of Mitoku Company. Kazama, a friend of macrobiotic teacher Michio Kushi, was looking for a supply of traditional shoyu for Kushi's students. Kushi's standards were very exact and could only be satisfied by high-quality, traditional shoyu. A few days later, when Sasaki showed Kazama his twelve 2,000-gallon cedar casks of naturally aging whole-soybean shoyu, Kazama knew his search was over.

At first, the Mitoku Company shipped the Sasaki family's traditional shoyu to the United States in wooden buckets. Today, this shoyu arrives at ports around the world in fifty-five-gallon drums, which have been loaded on twenty-foot-long sea containers. This precious cargo is welcomed by natural foods distributors who are proud to bottle Johsen shoyu under their private labels. In North America, you can find Johsen shoyu in natural foods stores under the Emperor's Kitchen, Koyo, Mitoku Macrobiotic, Tree of Life, and Westbrae labels.

TRADITIONAL OR HIGH-TECH?
THE DEBATE CONTINUES

It has been many years since our visit to the Sendai Shoyu and Miso Company. Jubei Sasaki has passed away, but his twelve casks of traditional shoyu have grown to 100, and his son continues the whole-soybean shoyu tradition. The debate over which shoyu is superior—the traditional or the high-tech—goes on. As the dollar's value continues to fall, the rising price of imported traditional shoyu is becoming less attractive to price-conscious shoppers who are looking for less expensive products. Fermentation technologists, supported by 99 percent of the shoyu industry, contend that the high-tech production methods are faster, more efficient, and produce a better shoyu at a lower price. Moreover, the soy oil extracted from soy meal can be sold as cooking oil rather than used to make soap, as in the traditional process. Traditional manufacturers counter that their shoyu has a richer bouquet and fuller flavor, so less is needed in seasoning. Also, most feel that hexane-extracted soy oil should not be used for cooking, and, in addition, that the industrial process used to distill hexane from petroleum is an environmental hazard.

For traditionalists like Jubei Sasaki, however, the issue is not the details of a process, but the deep feelings about a way of life. Traditional food manufacturers consider their work a craft, one that depends on a harmonious relationship with nature. Soaking food in harsh chemicals and creating an artificial environment in order to rush a natural process goes against their way of thinking. The fact that chemical laboratory analysis shows that both products are similar does not impress traditional manufacturers, who depend on intuitive understanding to make important decisions.

Ironically, a reverence for the old craft of making shoyu is shared by some high-tech shoyu giants, who consider the traditional process an important part of their history. At its corporate headquarters in Noda, Japan, Kikkoman Foods, Inc. maintains a traditional shoyu shop where whole-soybean moromi naturally ferments in immaculate hand-polished cedar casks. After pressing, the thick, rich traditional shoyu is bottled for Japan's royal family. In the emperor's kitchen, as well as in natural kitchens around the world, traditional does not necessarily mean old-fashioned.

COOKING WITH SHOYU

It's no wonder that shoyu has gained worldwide recognition as an outstanding and versatile seasoning. A few drops of this rich, dark fermented liquid brings out the natural sweetness and subtle hidden flavors in almost all foods, including fish, grains, vegetables, soups, sauces, and salads.

A complex chemical makeup gives traditional shoyu its extraordinary full flavor and irresistible aroma. Amino and fatty acids, released by the fermentation of whole soybeans, stimulate the taste buds and add a heartiness to meatless meals. Glutamic acid, a natural form of monosodium glutamate, makes traditional shoyu an excellent flavor-enhancer and tenderizer, perfect for marinating, pickling, and sautéeing. The fermentation of roasted cracked wheat yields natural sugars and alcohol, which impart a rich, savory aroma and subtle sweetness not found in tamari, shoyu's wheat-free cousin. With at least twenty identified flavor components, traditional shoyu can best be described by the term "deep-flavored."

In general, when using shoyu as a seasoning, it should be added during the last few minutes of cooking. Brief cooking enables it to harmonize with and heighten other flavors in the dish. In longer cooking, shoyu's slightly alcoholic qualities and delicate flavor are lost. When using shoyu to season soups, sauces, or sautées, a little sea salt can be added in the early stages of cooking to deepen the flavor of the ingredients. Shoyu should be added shortly before serving. A spray bottle is ideal for applying a light, even mist of shoyu to dishes such as sautées, fried rice or noodles, and steamed vegetables.

If you want to take full advantage of shoyu's rich bouquet and complement of flavors, there are several ways to use it uncooked. Combined with a little stock, mirin, and grated daikon or ginger, shoyu makes a delicious dip for tempura and other deep-fried foods, as well as for fish, pan-fried or baked mochi, and sushi. For a simple and tasty cold-weather pickle, cover thinly sliced or julienned rutabaga or carrots with a mixture of half shoyu and half water for two to four days. When the vegetables are pickled enough to have lost their raw taste, they should be refrigerated. Of course, shoyu can also be used as a table condiment.

To preserve the fine qualities of traditionally made shoyu, tighten the cap after each use and refrigerate or store in a cool, dark place. Heat, light, and air can oxidize shoyu, causing the flavor to deteriorate. Buying only a one-month supply at a time is another way to ensure your shoyu is in good condition.

A worker at the Sendai Shoyu and Miso Company places shoyu moromi into a cotton sack for pressing.

SHOYU RECIPES

Shoyu's delicate flavor is preferred over tamari's more assertive taste in the following recipes. Tamari, however, may be substituted if desired.

Vegetarian Noodle Soup

This hearty vegetable-noodle soup takes little time to prepare and really hits the spot on cold fall and winter days.

1 teaspoon light sesame oil
1 leek, halved lengthwise and diagonally cut into $1/4$-inch pieces
1 large carrot, halved lengthwise and diagonally cut into $1/8$-inch slices
$1/2$ teaspoon sea salt
6 cups Dashi (page 105) or vegetable stock
2 cups chopped kale or other green (loosely packed)
$1/2$ cup uncooked elbow noodles
2 tablespoons shoyu

Serves: 4

1. Heat oil in a large pot and sauté leek briefly. Add carrots and pinch of salt, and sauté. Add one cup dashi, cover, and cook 10 minutes.

2. Add remaining dashi and salt. Simmer 5 minutes.

3. Add greens, return soup to a simmer, then add noodles. Stir until soup returns to a simmer to prevent noodles from sticking to bottom of pot. Simmer, uncovered, until noodles are tender (7–10 minutes).

4. Add shoyu 1–2 minutes before end of cooking time. Serve hot.

Greens With Japanese Vinaigrette

Lightly cooked greens add vibrant color and concentrated nutrition to meals. The simple dressing in this recipe complements the slightly bitter flavor of the greens. Carrots and sesame seeds create an interesting contrast of color and texture.

1 large bunch leafy greens
(mustard, collards, kale, bok choy, turnips, etc.)
Pinch sea salt
½ medium carrot, cut into matchsticks
2 teaspoons toasted sesame oil
1 tablespoon brown rice vinegar
1 tablespoon plus one teaspoon shoyu
1 tablespoon sesame seeds, toasted

Serves: 4

1. Wash greens and remove tough stems from leaves.

2. Fill a large pot halfway with water and bring to a boil. Add sea salt and as many whole leaves as will comfortably fit. Boil greens until just tender (about 7 minutes for collards and kale, a little less for other greens).

3. When greens are tender, remove immediately and plunge into cold water to stop the cooking and hold the color. Drain, gently squeeze out excess water, and thinly slice. (If leaves are very large, cut in half lengthwise first.) Cook remaining leaves.

4. Boil carrots 2–3 minutes, remove, and cool under running water. Drain and set aside.

5. In a small bowl, whisk together sesame oil, vinegar, and shoyu.

6. In a mixing bowl, toss greens and carrots with dressing.

7. Place in a serving bowl, garnish with sesame seeds, and serve.

Marinated Tofu Medley

Marinated tofu turns a simple sautéed or stir-fried dish into a gourmet delight.

1 pound tofu
2 teaspoons light or toasted sesame oil
$\frac{1}{2}$ pound fresh mushrooms, sliced
Pinch sea salt
4 cups small broccoli florets

MARINADE
3 tablespoons mirin
2 tablespoons shoyu
2 tablespoons water or stock
1 clove garlic, finely minced (or 1 teaspoon fresh ginger juice)
2 teaspoons lemon juice (optional)

Serves: 4

1. Combine all marinade ingredients in a bowl and mix well.

2. Cut tofu into $\frac{1}{2}$-inch-thick slices and drain on paper towel. Next, cut tofu slices into 1 x 1 $\frac{1}{2}$-inch pieces and add to marinade. Let marinate in refrigerator for 30–60 minutes, turning occasionally.

3. Heat oil in a skillet, add mushrooms and salt, and sauté over medium heat 3 minutes.

4. Remove tofu from marinade and add to skillet along with broccoli. Toss gently, and add 2 tablespoons of marinade. Cover and simmer 5 minutes.

5. Turn off heat and remove cover immediately to prevent broccoli from losing its color. Serve hot.

Avocado "Sashimi"

Sashimi (raw fish) is a popular Japanese appetizer. Avocado's buttery texture and mild flavor are similar to some varieties of sashimi. As with sashimi, a dip of shoyu and pungent wasabi (Japanese horseradish) provides the perfect complement to avocado. This appetizer works best as the first course of a sit-down dinner. Its complex flavor awakens the taste buds and invites them into the meal.

1 small or medium-sized ripe (not overripe) avocado
Lemon juice for coating avocado slices
2 tablespoons shoyu
$\frac{1}{4}$ cup water
1 $\frac{1}{2}$ teaspoons wasabi powder

Serves: 6

1. Halve avocado lengthwise, slicing through to pit. Twist halves and pull apart. Remove the pit, then peel the avocado.

2. Thinly slice avocado halves lengthwise. (Unless peeled and sliced just before serving, coat slices lightly with lemon juice to prevent discoloration.) Arrange 3 slices on small individual dishes (sushi plates are ideal).

3. Combine soy sauce and water. Divide mixture among individual dip or condiment containers (about 1 tablespoon per serving).

4. Add one drop of water at a time to wasabi, and mix until it forms a thick paste.

5. Place small mound of wasabi on each plate of avocado "sashimi" for guests to add to dip. (For eye-appeal, place wasabi on very thin slice of red radish, or on a circle of overlapping radish slices.)

6. Pick up avocado slices with chopsticks, dip in shoyu, and enjoy.

TAMARI

The word tamari is often associated with one of the most confusing controversies of the modern natural foods movement. It all started when Western natural foods distributors began importing soy sauce from Japan. By accident, the distributors labeled the soy sauce "tamari," though it was actually high-quality shoyu. Years later, when distributors began importing authentic wheat-free tamari, they faced a dilemma. Most companies solved the problem by labeling the original product "shoyu" or "shoyu tamari," while labeling the new wheat-free product "tamari." But consumers are still confused. The simplest way to tell the difference between shoyu and tamari is to read the ingredients on the label. Shoyu contains wheat, while tamari is wheat-free.

In ancient times, tamari was simply the dark, rich liquid that pooled on the surface of fermenting miso. Tamari that is collected from miso dates back to eighth-century Japan and may have originated in China before the birth of Christ. By 1290, the first commercial tamari shop was established.

Gradually, central Japan, because of its ideal climate, choice soybeans, and high-quality water, became a tamari center. Around the fourteenth century, a wetter (purposely) soy miso was prepared; after fermentation, its flavorful liquid was pressed out, filtered, and bottled. This was the beginning of Japan's small tamari soy-sauce industry, which survives today in the Aichi, Mie, and Gifu prefectures. However, to cut costs, most of Japan's remaining tamari shops now use high-tech methods such as temperature-controlled fermentation; defatted soy meal is used rather than whole soybeans.

MAKING AUTHENTIC TAMARI

One of the few remaining authentic tamari shops is Mansan Brewing Company, founded by the Oguri family in 1875. Located in the small town of Handa, on the Chita peninsula in the Aichi prefecture, the Oguri shop is a virtual soy-sauce museum. Inside the old wooden storehouse, rows of towering 100-year-old wooden casks, held together with huge hoops of braided bamboo, are filled to capacity with 30,000 pounds of thick, rich tamari. The air is filled with the heady aroma of fermenting soy sauce, and, if you listen carefully, you can hear the sound of bubbling brew, particularly on hot summer nights.

Although the Oguri family has bought some new equipment for washing, cooking, and mixing, fourth-generation president Enichiro Oguri contends whole natural ingredients, hand-made koji, and long, natural aging in wood are still his company's proud hallmarks.

In the fall, when natural conditions are ideal for making koji, the Oguris begin each day by soaking one thousand pounds of choice organic soybeans in well water. The next morning, the swollen beans are placed in a one-ton capacity steamer. After cooking, the soft beans are crushed into tiny balls (about $\frac{5}{8}$ inch in diameter) called *miso dama*. These balls are dusted with a mixture of *Aspergillus* mold spores and roasted barley flour and then placed in a special room to incubate for forty-eight hours. During this time, Oguri carefully controls the temperature and humidity.

The sweet smelling, fluffy, pale yellow balls, now called *koji*, are removed from the incubator and placed on bamboo mats to dry for two weeks. The Mansan shop is the only tamari company that uses this unique koji drying process. According to Enichiro Oguri, this process is responsible for Mansan tamari's extra thick, rich quality and concentrated flavor.

The dried koji is mixed with a brine solution (sea salt and water) and placed in ten-foot-tall cedar vats to ferment. This fermenting mash, called *moromi*, is actually a thick paste that, like miso, is pressed with 1,000 pounds of river stones.

During the long aging process, enzymes from the *Aspergillus* mold in the koji and naturally occurring yeasts and bacteria—which inhabit Mansan's old storage building—slowly break down the moromi. The complex carbohydrates, proteins, and oils of the soybeans are transformed into sweet sugars, aromatic alcohol, and flavorful amino and fatty acids. The mature fermented moromi is then placed in cotton sacks and pressed under great force to extract its dark liquid, a mixture of tamari and crude soy oil. The oil, which rises to the surface, is removed. The tamari is finally ready for settling, low-temperature pasteurization, and bottling. The entire process takes about eighteen months.

Mansan tamari, which is sold in the United States under the Mitoku Macrobiotic and Emperor's Kitchen labels, is found in most well-stocked natural foods stores.

A FIGHT FOR SURVIVAL

The Mansan Brewing Company was almost completely destroyed in September of 1959 by the fierce Ise-wan typhoon, which took 5,000 lives on the Chita Peninsula. Enichiro, who was forty-four at the time, remembers fifteen-foot-tall waves pounding Handa as sea water flooded the Mansan shop. The water rose to a depth of almost five feet while employees worked through the night to stem the flood. In the morning, Oguri's worst fears were confirmed. Much of the company's assets were lost. The following years were very difficult for the Oguri family, but gradually they recovered.

Each ten-foot-tall cedar vat of fermenting tamari is mixed daily.

In 1982 Akiyoshi Kazama, president of Mitoku Company, Japan's largest exporter of natural soy sauce, discovered Mansan tamari. Kazama had been searching Japan for traditionally made soy sauce for the macrobiotic community at the request of macrobiotic teacher Michio Kushi. And it was in 1982 that the governor of Aichi gave the Oguris a coveted award for having the best tamari in the prefecture. Today, thirty years after the flood, the Oguris are very surprised and grateful to find their soy sauce being sold on five continents, where Mansan tamari is considered a macrobiotic staple.

COOKING WITH TAMARI

Tamari is a uniquely delicious, versatile seasoning that adds immeasurably to the flavor of soups, sauces, vegetables, dips, and entrées. Making tamari is an expensive, time-consuming process. However, because tamari is made with 100 percent whole soybeans, it is very concentrated, so a little goes a long way. The Oguri's special koji drying process, described earlier, further concentrates the flavor. Tamari's "staying power" during cooking is incredible. Reduce the amount of soy sauce called for in a recipe by about 25 percent when cooking with tamari.

Unlike shoyu, which derives much of its flavor from the natural alcohol produced by wheat fermentation, tamari's rich flavor comes from an abundance of amino acids, which are derived from soy protein. Because amino acids are not volatile, they don't evaporate the way alcohol does. This makes tamari the better soy sauce to choose when lengthy cooking is required. Tamari also contains more flavor-intensifying glutamic acid than shoyu. Bland foods like shiitake mushrooms and tofu are enhanced when simmered in a seasoned liquid. For dishes that require this long-simmering process, tamari is the preferred seasoning.

You may have noticed that alcohol is listed as an ingredient in new domestic brands of soy sauce. Concentrated ethyl alcohol is sometimes used as a soy-sauce preservative. According to Japanese fermentation experts, traditional shoyu made with koji that contains 50 percent wheat and 50 percent whole soybeans produces enough alcohol from wheat fermentation (about 2.5 percent) to inhibit the growth of yeast. Traditional tamari, however, contains no wheat and produces only about 0.1 percent natural alcohol. To prevent the growth of yeast after the bottle is opened, some tamari producers add concentrated ethyl alcohol before packaging.

Mansan tamari contains no added ethyl alcohol. At great expense, the Oguri family adds a little of Japan's finest rice "brandy," Mikawa mirin (Chapter 2), to their tamari. Mikawa mirin is made by the same traditional koji process as Mansan tamari. The addition of mirin, not only prevents the growth of yeast, but actually contributes to the aroma and deep, rich taste of Mansan tamari.

TAMARI RECIPES

Tamari's staying power during lengthy cooking makes it ideally suited for the following recipes, though shoyu may be substituted.

Simmered Buttercup Squash

This simple dish works equally well with butternut squash or Hokkaido pumpkin.

3-inch-piece kombu
1 small or ½ large buttercup squash,
seeded and cut into bite-sized chunks
Water
Pinch sea salt
1–2 teaspoons tamari

Serves: 4

1. Place kombu in bottom of a medium-sized saucepan, top with squash chunks, add water to almost cover, and bring to a simmer.

2. Add salt and tamari, and simmer gently until chunks are tender.

3. Remove squash from broth with slotted spoon and serve.

Tofu Cutlets

Here's an easy and inexpensive entrée that doesn't compromise flavor or nutrition.

1 block tofu (approximately 1 pound)
2 ½ tablespoons tamari
1 tablespoon whole wheat flour
2 tablespoons cornmeal
1 ½ tablespoons sesame or canola oil
1 tablespoon dry white wine or sake (optional)
2 teaspoons mirin
(if omitting wine or sake, increase mirin to 1 ½ tablespoons)
1 scallion, minced
1 rounded teaspoon peeled and finely grated ginger

Serves: 4

1. Cut tofu lengthwise into 4 slices. To remove excess moisture from tofu, wrap slices in a clean, dry kitchen towel and place on wooden cutting board. Place a 2–3 pound weight on top and leave for 20–30 minutes.

2. Place 1 tablespoon tamari in a bowl or plate. Gently roll tofu slices in tamari to coat all sides. Drain excess tamari.

3. Combine flour and cornmeal, and roll tofu in mixture.

4. Heat oil in a skillet, and fry tofu over medium heat until crisp and golden on both sides.

5. Combine remaining 1½ tablespoons tamari, wine or sake (if using), and mirin. Pour sauce over tofu, then remove skillet from heat.

6. Use individual bowls or plates for serving. For an attractive presentation, garnish each slice with minced scallion and, if desired, finely grated ginger. Spoon remaining liquid from pan around cutlets. Serve hot.

Burdock Kinpira

Burdock root has long been prized in the Orient for its pleasant, crunchy texture and earthy flavor, as well as for its medicinal qualities. It is highly regarded in Oriental medicine as a blood purifier. The long, slender cultivated burdock roots are available in better supermarkets and natural foods stores. Burdock grows wild almost everywhere in this country, except the southernmost states. (The large, heart-shaped green leaves and thick stalks resemble rhubarb.)

This adaptation of a traditional Japanese recipe is our family's favorite way to enjoy burdock, especially during the late fall and winter months.

3 burdock roots (each approximately 12 inches long)

2 large carrots, cut into julienne strips

2–3 teaspoons light or toasted sesame oil

$\frac{1}{4}$ teaspoon sea salt

2 tablespoons mirin

1 tablespoon tamari

Pinch cayenne pepper or Japanese 7-spice (optional)

Serves: 4

1. Scrub burdock well, and cut into very thin, 2-inch-long julienne strips. Immediately submerge strips in cold water to prevent discoloring.

2. Heat oil in a skillet or heavy saucepan. Add drained burdock, and sauté over medium heat several minutes.

3. Add water, if necessary, to prevent scorching. Cover and cook over medium-low heat 10–15 minutes, or until burdock is nearly tender.

4. Add carrots, salt, and one tablespoon mirin. Sauté briefly. Cover and let cook. Check often to be sure vegetables are not sticking to bottom of pan.

5. When liquid in skillet is absorbed, add one tablespoon tamari, another tablespoon mirin, and pinch of cayenne pepper or Japanese 7-spice (if desired). Toss, cover, and cook briefly until tender, adding 2 tablespoons water if necessary.

6. Transfer to a bowl and serve hot.

Broiled Marinated Snapper

The use of tamari in marinating takes advantage of its qualities as both flavor enhancer and tenderizer.

1–1 ⅓ *pounds fresh snapper fillets*
(can substitute cod, sole, haddock, or grouper)
Pinch cayenne pepper (optional)
3–4 lemon wedges
Parsley sprigs or watercress for garnish

MARINADE
2 tablespoons tamari
¼ cup dry white wine or sake
1 tablespoon extra virgin olive oil or sesame oil
1 tablespoon lemon juice
1 clove garlic, finely minced
1 teaspoon peeled and finely grated ginger

Serves: 3–4

1. Rinse fish under cold running water, then pat dry.

2. Combine marinade ingredients in a pie plate or baking pan.

3. Lay fish in marinade, then turn over. (This coats the top of fillets while other side is marinating.) If desired, lightly sprinkle with cayenne. Marinate 15 minutes, then turn over.

4. Sprinkle with a little more cayenne (if using) and marinate 15 minutes more. Occasionally spoon marinade over top of fish.

5. Preheat broiler.

6. Remove fish from the marinade and place on oiled baking sheet. Reserve marinade.

7. Broil fish on one side about 5 minutes. Turn fish, spoon a little marinade on top, and broil about 3 minutes more. (Broiling time will vary according to thickness of fish. If still translucent at the center, cook a few minutes more and check again.)

8. Serve hot. If desired, sprinkle teaspoon or two of marinade over each serving. Garnish with lemon wedge and sprig of parsley or watercress.

10

TEA

A National Institution

Both stimulating and relaxing, Japanese teas such as tangy *sencha*, smoky *hojicha*, and earthy *kukicha* refresh the palate and heighten the pleasure of eating all types of food. Although all Japanese tea comes from the evergreen *Camellia sinensis*, unique processing produces teas with different tastes, colors, and physiological effects. Like many herbal brews, Japanese tea has legendary health benefits, some now scientifically proven (see *The Healing Properties of Tea*, page 136).

Originally a medicinal beverage brought from ancient China by Buddhist monks, tea *(cha)* was both rare and expensive in Japan for many centuries. The first tea seeds were planted in Japan during China's T'ang dynasty (618–905), and cultivation of the plants was associated with temple life and religious activity. Today, a thousand years later, tea has become Japan's national beverage. From *cha-no-yu*, the Zen Buddhist tea ceremony, to *o-cha*, the daily three o'clock tea break, drinking tea is a Japanese institution.

NAGATA TEA GARDEN

Our love affair with Japanese tea began during our extensive visit to Japan several years ago. Upon returning home, we were relieved to learn that some of Japan's finest teas, which are grown around the town of Uji, were available in the United States. Uji is located on the old road between the ancient capitals of Nara and Kyoto, about 230 miles southwest of Tokyo. Uji's rich, slightly acidic soil is ideal for growing tea. Early morning mist from the Uji river moistens the leaves of the plants and shields them from the sun. Following the natural contours of the valleys and surrounding hills, Uji's landscape is patched with three- and four-acre tea fields. Straight rows of smooth, tightly trimmed bushes look more like ornamental hedges than individual tea plants.

Off the main road, on a hill overlooking Uji, the manicured look of the plantations below gives way to fields of lumpy, irregular rows of tea plants—the remote, centuries-old tea plantation of the Nagata family. Since 1974, it has supplied most of the organic sencha, hojicha, and kukicha teas to natural foods shops around the world.

Following the principles of an agricultural method known as nature farming, the Nagatas have been a curiosity to their tea-farming neighbors. Most tea farmers spray their plants with chemicals fifteen to twenty times a year, but the Nagata family has rejected chemical agriculture completely. They do not use animal manures, chemical fertilizers, herbicides, or pesticides—they replenish the nutrients in their topsoil with vegetable-quality compost only. Nature farming stresses the importance of building soil vitality by maintaining a semi-wild natural environment. Plants are not overly protected or pampered but are allowed to fend for themselves with the help of a strong, balanced topsoil.

Company president Aijiro Nagata insists that it is not necessary to prune tea bushes uniformly. "Each bush," he says, "should be allowed to grow according to its own pattern." Although he harvests a little less tea than similar-sized farms that use chemical methods, his plants have far less mold and blight. Also, the Nagata tea plants usually produce tea leaves for twice as long a period of time as plants that have been chemically treated. Chemically treated tea plants generally burn themselves out in about twenty years, but Nagata plants commonly produce for forty years, some for as long as one hundred.

In early spring, Uji farmers cover their tender tea leaves with dark netting or slotted bamboo screens to protect them from the afternoon sun. These first spring leaves are processed into gyokuro ("jewel dew"), Japan's rarest, most expensive tea. Steamed, dried, and ground to a fine powder, these early leaves become matcha, the jade green tea of the ancient tea ceremony.

Unlike their neighbors, in the spring, the Nagatas process their most prized leaves into sencha, a high-quality green tea offered to house guests and served at fine Japanese restaurants. Sencha goes especially well with sushi and sashimi (raw fish) as it is said to aid in the digestion of fish oil and protein.

To make sencha, the freshly picked tender leaves are immediately steamed for a minute or so. Steaming softens the leaves and turns them a delicate emerald green color. (The steaming process prevents the tea from fermenting and turning dark. This distinguishes Japanese tea from partially fermented oolong and fully fermented black English teas.) Once steamed, the leaves are rolled into thin curls, dried slowly in ovens, cooled, and immediately packed to seal in their fresh taste and aroma. Slightly bittersweet sencha, more than any other tea, has the fresh taste of just-picked leaves.

The Nagatas continue to pick sencha throughout the spring. By late June or July the leaves are too large and coarse to qualify as sencha and are processed into hojicha. These leaves are steamed, mixed with black volcanic sand, and roasted in revolving ovens. The sand, later removed, helps the leaves roast slowly and evenly. Roasting further neutralizes the leaves' already weak astringent and stimulating qualities (tea leaves lose caffeine strength as they grow), so both children and adults can drink hojicha any time of the day. Hojicha is one of the Nagata family's most popular teas.

In Japan, coarse summer leaves are usually not roasted, but are sold as lower-quality green tea called bancha. This is the mild, yellow-green tea served in many Japanese restaurants around the world. Within the American natural foods world, however, bancha has quite a different meaning. It has become associated with a popular tea made from roasted twigs and very coarse leaves. Often referred to as kukicha, roasted twig tea is little known in modern Japan.

In Japan, kukicha has been stigmatized as "a poor man's drink," because, like brown rice, it brings back memories of the days of deprivation during and after World War II. Macrobiotics founder George Ohsawa introduced kukicha to the West forty years ago. Since it contains only one-tenth the caffeine of sencha and because it is the most alkalinizing Japanese tea, Ohsawa considered it to be the most balanced beverage. Indeed, kukicha is an excellent complement to the grain-based, mostly vegetarian diet he advocated.

The Nagatas are amused at the demand for their poor-man's tea but are happy to have a market for the twigs and leaves they might otherwise use as mulch. However, the time-consuming, labor-intense methods used to make kukicha adds substantially to its cost.

The Nagatas keep the caffeine level in kukicha as low as possible by selecting only older twigs and harvesting them in fall and winter when caffeine is naturally lowest. Twigs are steamed, dried, and stored in paper bags for two to three years in order to develop the best flavor. After aging, twigs are cut and graded to size. Each grade is then roasted separately at different temperatures and lengths of time

The Healing Properties of Tea

Years ago, the Chinese boiled their water to guard against bacterial contamination. Some historians believe that tea leaves were first used to flavor this boiled water. Gradually, over thousands of years, extraordinary healing powers became associated with tea. Sixteenth-century European explorers, who encountered tea for the first time in the Orient, reported that it was a hot, medicinal drink used to relieve fever, headache, stomachache, and joint pain.

Although caffeine has received bad press in the West, it might have been this very quality in tea, which instantly invigorates the body, that attracted early religious leaders and physicians. Scientists have identified caffeine as one of a potent group of drugs called methylxanthines found in over sixty plant species. Caffeine blocks adenosine, a natural tranquilizer, so the brain is overstimulated, heightening intellectual activity. The highest quality Japanese green teas, which are picked from tender spring leaves high in caffeine, may have three or four times the caffeine of coffee. But their high tannin and vitamin-C content is believed to moderate the stimulating effect. This synergistic quality of vitamin C and tannin with caffeine may explain why Zen monks use green tea during long meditations to stay alert but calm.

Other side effects of caffeine, such as widening of the arteries and pulmonary vessels, increasing blood flow to the heart, and stimulating kidney and bladder functions, were viewed as medicinal effects by ancient healers, who used green tea with moderation.

Caffeine aside, the wealth of traditional folklore associated with Japanese green tea has led some Japanese scientists to study its effect on the body. Researchers in Japan claim that pregnant women should drink green tea because it contains zinc, which is important during pregnancy. According to another study, because of tea's natural tannins and fluorides, a cup of tea a day for children can cut the number of reported cavities in half. Tannin, an astringent responsible for green tea's bitter taste, is also thought to help the body discharge toxins due to pollution, and to accelerate the metabolism of fats.

Recent Japanese research has shown that flavonoid, a yellow pigment found in green tea, may prevent the formation of some forms of cataracts. It may also control the agglutination of blood platelets, which indicates that it may be effective in preventing blood clots and strokes.

Recent chemical analysis has revealed that green tea contains significant amounts of water-soluble vitamins and minerals. Because green tea leaves are steamed immediately after they are picked, their most oxidative enzymes are destroyed, so they retain their green color and natural vitamin and mineral content.

to ensure uniformity. Finally, the twigs are blended and packaged. The Nagata formula for just the right ratio of twig size and age is a carefully guarded family secret. But the rich taste of their twig tea is no secret—Nagata kukicha is the most popular Japanese tea in the natural foods market.

Recently, the Nagatas developed brown rice kukicha, an equal blend of roasted organic brown rice and tea twigs, which is available under the Mitoku Macrobiotic label. The delightful, nutty flavor imparted by the roasted rice makes this an especially delicious and satisfying tea, both hot and chilled.

Robbie Swinnerton, a British food writer who has lived in Asia for over ten years, claims that different teas complement different diets. "Hojicha and kukicha," says Swinnerton, "are appropriate for a grain-based, mostly vegetarian diet, whereas the typical Japanese fish-based diet is well balanced by green tea. The more meat- and poultry-based Chinese diet features fermented or semifermented red or oolong teas, and the British tradition of meat dishes three times a day calls for the dark, fermented teas of India."

SHOPPING FOR JAPANESE TEA

The best place to shop for high-quality Japanese teas is in natural foods stores. Nagata's organic teas are available in North America under the Mitoku Macrobiotic, Koyo, Choice, and Haiku labels.

Brown rice tea is another traditional Japanese beverage found in both natural foods and Oriental food stores. Also called *genmai cha*, it is a mixture of tea leaves and roasted brown rice. Served both hot and chilled, brown rice tea has a mild, nutty flavor.

You do not have to stop drinking coffee to enjoy Japanese tea. Mixing coffee and kukicha (half and half) creates a robust morning brew with half the caffeine. We enjoy Japanese teas straight. Properly brewed, they are deeply satisfying.

Kukicha Tonics

Kukicha, thought to be useful as a blood purifier and alkalinizing agent, is the foundation for two important tonics. These potent remedies rarely fail to bring quick relief.

Rejuvenating Tonic

Taken warm, this soothing drink helps combat fatigue, improve circulation, aid digestion, and relieve hangovers.

1 cup kukicha tea (see page 139)
½ shredded umeboshi plum, or ½ teaspoon paste
Few drops shoyu
Few drops fresh ginger juice

1. Bring kukicha tea to a boil, then remove from heat.
2. Add umeboshi, shoyu, and ginger juice.
3. Steep 1–2 minutes before drinking.

Relief Tonic

This drink helps relieve diarrhea, stomach hyperacidity, and indigestion.

1 cup kukicha tea (see page 139)
1 heaping teaspoon crushed kuzu
1–2 tablespoons water
1 shredded umeboshi plum, or 1 teaspoon paste
½–1 teaspoon shoyu

1. Prepare kukicha tea. Set aside to cool.
2. Dissolve kuzu in water.
3. Add kuzu and umeboshi to cooled tea. Bring to a boil, stirring constantly until thick. Reduce heat and simmer 1–2 minutes.
4. Add shoyu, stir, and sip.

ART OF TEA BREWING

The art of Japanese tea preparation and presentation involves paying attention to water temperature, steeping time, and serving methods. If the water is hotter than required, the delicate taste of green tea might be lost; steeping too long can produce teas that are dark and bitter. The Japanese traditionally serve sencha in small delicate tea cups; hojicha, kukicha, and brown rice tea are generally served in larger, handle-less mugs. Tea is never served with sugar or milk—if sweetness is desired, a little rice syrup can be added.

Kukicha and brown rice-kukicha are the easiest Japanese teas to brew. Unlike other varieties, which are never boiled, kukicha is simmered to extract the full flavor from its twigs. Simply add three level tablespoons of kukicha to one quart of water, bring to a boil, and simmer gently for three to five minutes. Pour the tea through a strainer into the cups, and dump the twigs back into the pot. The twigs can be used once again, but a few fresh twigs may need to be added for full-bodied flavor. If you are using kukicha or brown rice-kukicha tea bags, steep one tea bag in one cup of boiling water for five to six minutes. Serve hot or chilled—with lemon if you prefer. For a refreshing summer drink, combine chilled kukicha with an equal portion of apple juice.

Hojicha and sencha are closely related, and are brewed in the same way. Because sencha contains more caffeine, however, it is served in smaller quantities, and is never used to quench one's thirst. A large teapot is useful if you are serving more than two people. Warm the teapot by filling it with hot water. Pour the water out and add one level tablespoon of tea for each cup of water you will be boiling. In another pot, bring cold, pure water to a full boil, then immediately remove it from the heat. Let the water sit a minute before pouring it over the tea leaves or tea bag in the warmed pot. Allow the tea to steep for only a minute, or it will become bitter. If you are using bulk tea, strain it as it is poured into the cups. Alternate pouring a little tea into each cup, until the pot is completely drained. This pouring method will insure each person's tea to be about the same strength. The leaves may be reused once or twice. For both sencha and hojicha, fresh leaves should not be added to used ones—discard spent leaves, rinse the pot, and begin fresh. Unlike sencha, which becomes bitter when cooled, hojicha makes a delicious and refreshing cool summer beverage.

Sencha, hojicha, and kukicha are available in good-quality tea bags and in bulk. However, if stored improperly, these teas can become stale quickly. Buy no more than a one-month supply at a time, and keep it stored in an airtight container in a cool, dry place.

11

SNOW-DRIED TOFU
Protein Powerhouse

I n winter, high in the mountains of central Japan, Aki Takagi's small family shop is busy making one of the world's most concentrated sources of high-quality vegetable protein. Six times as concentrated as regular tofu, snow-dried tofu has twice the protein of fish, beef, and chicken, and none of the cholesterol. What's more, with a full complement of essential amino acids, the quality of its protein is comparable to that of meat and dairy foods. Snow-dried tofu is also a concentrated source of iron, calcium, and phosphorus.

Nutrition aside, Takagi's snow-dried tofu may be the original convenience food. The 2 x 2 ½-inch pieces are reconstituted when briefly soaked in plain water. Like a sponge, this food is ready to pick up the flavor of seasonings, sauces, and marinades. It cooks in minutes and is delicious when simmered, sautéed, or deep-fried. Snow-dried tofu adds interest, flavor, and nutrition to any style of cooking.

PRESERVING A CENTURIES-OLD PROCESS

Starting each year on a cold, crisp December morning, Aki Takagi begins his ancient five-hundred-year-old process by cooking stone-ground soybeans in a cauldron to make a firm tofu. This *kata-dofu* (hard tofu) is a traditional favorite of high mountain people who prefer its coarse texture and rich taste to "bland, watery, lowland varieties," as they say.

The fresh tofu is cooled in icy well water and skillfully cut into thin slabs. These slabs are placed on bamboo trays and allowed to freeze overnight. The water in the tofu—about 86 percent by weight—turns to ice. The protein, minerals, and other solids congeal into a firm, lacy network. The following morning, workers begin the tedious task of stringing pieces of frozen tofu with braided rice straw. Takagi-san remembers a time when snow-dried tofu producers would gather the village children to string the tofu squares. "It was quite a sight to see their small, agile hands do this work so swiftly and skillfully," he recollects. Now, as then, the task is completed by late afternoon. Immediately, workers facilitate the freeze-drying process by hanging the tied frozen tofu from wooden frames in an open shed. There the tofu squares are left to twist and sway in the wind. During the day, temperatures are just warm enough to thaw the tofu and evaporate some of the water. At night, the tofu freezes solid again. This "aging" process is critical, and only temperature and humidity that fall within a narrow range can produce the finely textured, highly absorbent, snow-dried tofu that is characteristic of this region of Japan. After about twenty days, the tofu slices are feather-light and bone-dry. Only 10 percent of the original moisture remains, and nature's low-tech drying process is complete.

AN ACCIDENTAL DISCOVERY

Like many traditional Japanese food manufacturers, the Takagi family owes its unique way of life to its Chinese neighbors. According to William Shurtleff, co-author with Akiko Aoyagi of several books on traditional Japanese foods, frozen tofu was probably first made in the cold mountainous regions of northern China about 1,000 to 1,500 years ago. It was found that if tofu was left out in the snow overnight until frozen solid, it underwent a radical transformation. When later placed in warm water, the tofu thawed, leaving a fine-grained, highly absorbent food that had the texture of tender meat.

Although Chinese frozen tofu had vast culinary potential, it had two drawbacks. First, it had to remain frozen or, like fresh tofu, it would spoil due to bacterial action. Second, like ice, it was heavy and difficult to transport.

Leave it to the Japanese to make a good thing better. About 1225 A.D., in a temple on Mount Koya, near Kyoto, a Buddhist monk began drying frozen tofu in a heated shed. This new "dried food" came to be known as *koya dofu*. Because it contained little water, it kept for several months without spoiling. The relentlessly utilitarian Japanese mind, however, was still not satisfied. In the fifteenth century, aggressive warlord Takeda Shingen recognized koya dofu's potential as a military ration. To make the process more mobile, Shingen did away with the heated shed and simply let the frozen tofu dry in the sun for a few weeks. This *kori* (frozen) *dofu*, named thus to distinguish it from the monk's version, was virtually imperishable.

SHOPPING FOR SNOW-DRIED TOFU

The kori-dofu, or snow-dried tofu, found today in most natural foods stores is made just as Takeda Shingen made it over five centuries ago. According to Chris Dawson of Mitoku Company, Ltd. (Japan's largest exporter of natural kori-dofu), less than 1 percent of Japan's kori-dofu is now produced by the natural "snow-dried" method. In the early 1900s, manufacturers began using quick, artificial freezing and drying techniques. Soon, additives such as baking soda and ammonia were being used to make mass-produced kori-dofu softer, less brittle, and pristine white. Today, most of the natural kori-dofu is made by a few surviving manufacturers grouped together around the shores of Lake Suwa in the mountains of the frigid Nagano prefecture. Takagi is one of those traditional producers.

COOKING WITH SNOW-DRIED TOFU

With its porous, firm yet tender texture and its mild, unimposing taste, dried tofu has an amazing ability to absorb the flavors of the foods and seasonings it is cooked with. Unlike fresh tofu, which tends to break apart when sautéed, dried tofu holds its shape even after prolonged cooking. These qualities make it well-suited to any style of cooking. Appropriately seasoned, it can be used in place of meat or poultry in many ethnic entrées. Lightweight and easy to store and prepare, it is also the ideal camp food.

Before snow-dried tofu can be used, it must first be reconstituted. Briefly soaking this food in plain water, then squeezing out most of the moisture is all that is needed. Once reconstituted, there are three basic ways of cooking with snow-dried tofu. Familiarize yourself with these versatile techniques. First, snow-dried tofu can be diced and added directly to well-seasoned broths, sauces, or other flavorful dishes. The second method is to marinate the diced tofu for thirty minutes. A marinade of natural soy sauce, mirin, and ginger is perfect when making Oriental entrées. Soy sauce, white wine, and herbs associated with Western cuisines, such as poultry seasoning or rosemary and bay leaf, impart a flavor suited to Western dishes. The third—and most versatile—method is to simmer the tofu in a well-seasoned broth. It may then be served as is; pan-fried in toasted sesame oil; or diced and added to stews, sautées, grains, sauces, and salads. Simmered snow-dried tofu is especially good when it is deep-fried after being dipped in tempura batter, or after being dipped in egg batter and rolled in bread crumbs.

Coarsely grating dried tofu before reconstituting yields another range of possibilities. Try adding some to stuffings, casseroles, and vegetable or grain-based burgers or croquettes.

Dried tofu stores well for several months, but it gradually turns yellow-brown with age, so buy only light beige-colored dried tofu, and store it in a cool, dry place away from direct sunlight. To reconstitute, soak dried tofu in warm water for five minutes, then press firmly between your hands. Repeatedly dampen and press until the liquid that comes out is no longer milky.

SNOW-DRIED TOFU RECIPES

The following recipes use snow-dried tofu in many styles of cooking. Try a few and you will soon be thinking of new ways to incorporate this convenient, concentrated food into your daily meals.

Snow-Dried Tofu With Ginger

Snow-dried tofu is delicious when simmered in a shoyu-seasoned broth and served with grated ginger and a garnish of slivered scallion. Several recipes start by flavoring dried tofu this way before adding it to other ingredients to make sauces, stews, or sautées. By using different herbs and seasonings in the broth, you can flavor the dried tofu in ways appropriate to the dish you plan to use it in. Try the recipes below to get the idea, then experiment with your own creations.

6 pieces snow-dried tofu

1 cup water

1–1 $\frac{1}{3}$ tablespoons shoyu or tamari (to taste)

1 tablespoon mirin

1 clove garlic, pressed or finely minced,
or 2 thin slices peeled fresh ginger (optional)

1 $\frac{1}{2}$ teaspoons peeled and finely grated ginger

Slivered scallion for garnish

Serves: 3

1. Reconstitute dried tofu by soaking it in lukewarm water 5 minutes. Repeatedly dampen and squeeze out excess water until liquid that comes out is no longer milky.

2. Press cakes until fairly dry, then place in a saucepan or skillet with water, shoyu, mirin, and garlic or ginger. Simmer, loosely covered, until most liquid is absorbed (15–20 minutes). Be careful not to scorch tofu.

3. Serve with small mound of grated ginger and a sprinkling of scallion.

VARIATION

-   After simmering, pan-fry the tofu in 2–3 teaspoons toasted sesame oil until slightly browned on both sides. Serve as shown above or use in other recipes.

Tofu in a Blanket

This protein-rich entrée is both delicious and satisfying.

6 pieces snow-dried tofu
6 whole cabbage leaves
Pinch sea salt

FOR SIMMERING TOFU
1 cup water
1–1 ⅓ tablespoons shoyu or tamari
1 tablespoon mirin
3 thin slices peeled fresh ginger root (optional)

FOR SIMMERING STUFFED CABBAGE
⅔ cup water
2 teaspoons shoyu or tamari
½ bay leaf
Pinch rosemary

Serves: 3

1. Reconstitute dried tofu by soaking in lukewarm water 5 minutes. Repeatedly dampen and squeeze out excess water until liquid that comes out is no longer milky.

2. Press cakes fairly dry and place in saucepan or skillet with water, shoyu or tamari, mirin, and ginger (if using). Simmer, loosely covered, until most liquid is absorbed (15–20 minutes). Be careful not to scorch tofu.

3. In a large pot, bring 2 inches of water to boil. Add salt and cabbage leaves. Parboil 5 minutes. Remove leaves, cool immediately under running water or in a cold-water bath, and drain. If central ribs are stiff, cut them out.

4. Cut each piece of tofu in half. Stack two halves in the center of each cabbage leaf. Neatly wrap (as you would a package) and fasten with toothpicks.

5. Combine last four ingredients in medium-sized skillet, add cabbage parcels, cover, and simmer 20 minutes. Serve hot.

New England Boiled Dinner

Snow-dried tofu replaces corned beef as the concentrated source of protein in this classic winter one-pot meal. Serve with whole grain bread or other grain of your choice for a simple, warming, and delicious dinner.

6 pieces snow-dried tofu

2 cups kombu stock, vegetable stock, or water

2 tablespoons tamari or shoyu

1 tablespoon mirin

1 bay leaf

Pinch of rosemary

1 onion, cut into 8–12 wedges

3 carrots, cut into bite-sized chunks

1 rib celery, cut on the diagonal into 2-inch lengths

10–12 mushrooms, halved or quartered

3 wedges buttercup squash (1-inch pieces),
or several ½-inch slices butternut squash

12 broccoli florets

Serves: 3

1. Reconstitute dried tofu by soaking it in lukewarm water 5 minutes. Repeatedly dampen and squeeze out excess water until liquid that comes out is no longer milky.

2. Cut tofu pieces in half lengthwise, then cut each half crosswise into thirds.

3. In a large skillet, bring one cup stock or water to a simmer with tamari and mirin. Add bay leaf, rosemary, onion, and tofu. Cover and simmer 10 minutes.

4. Add remaining cup of stock or water, carrots, celery, and mushrooms. Cover and simmer 5 minutes. Add squash and simmer until vegetables are nearly tender (about 10 minutes).

5. If pan is nearly dry, add ⅓ cup water mixed with 1 teaspoon shoyu. Add broccoli and simmer until tender-crisp (about 5 minutes).

6. Place skillet in center of table, uncover, and serve.

Setsuko's Dofu-Carrot Sandwich

This tasty treat comes from Setsuko Dawson, expert macrobiotic cooking instructor.

12 pieces snow-dried tofu
2 large carrots
2 cups Dashi (page 105)
2 tablespoons shoyu
1 tablespoon mirin
Vegetable oil for deep-frying
3 sheets nori
3 tablespoons unbleached wheat flour
Pinch of sea salt

Serves: 4

1. Reconstitute tofu by soaking it in lukewarm water 5 minutes. Repeatedly dampen and squeeze out excess water until liquid that comes out is no longer milky.

2. Cut carrots on the diagonal into slices that are about the same length and thickness as the whole pieces of reconstituted tofu.

3. In a medium-sized pot, add shoyu and mirin to dashi. Add carrots and tofu. Simmer 15 minutes.

4. Remove carrots. Continue to simmer tofu 10 minutes or until all liquid is absorbed.

5. Fill a deep pot with 2 inches of oil and heat to 350°F.

6. While oil is heating, cut nori sheets in half along fold. In a small bowl, mix flour and salt with enough water to form a thick paste. Sandwich one slice of carrot between two squares of tofu, and wrap with strip of nori. Seal both ends with flour paste.

7. Deep-fry in hot oil 1–2 minutes, turning once. Remove from pot and drain on absorbent paper.

8. Cut each "sandwich" into 2 or 3 pieces and serve hot.

Chinese-Style Snow-Dried Tofu and Vegetables

A wok is ideal for making this dish, but a large skillet is fine, also. Feel free to vary the vegetables used for this recipe according to the season and to whatever ingredients you have on hand. Serve over udon or bifun noodles, millet, couscous, or rice.

3 pieces snow-dried tofu

2 tablespoons sesame oil

1 teaspoon toasted sesame oil

1 onion, thinly sliced

2 large carrots, cut into 2-inch-long julienne strips

Pinch of sea salt

2 ribs celery, thinly sliced on the diagonal

1 green bell pepper, thinly sliced

7–8 large mushrooms, sliced

2 teaspoons crushed kuzu

1/3 cup water or stock

ORIENTAL MARINADE

2 tablespoons shoyu

3 tablespoons mirin

2 tablespoons stock or water

2 teaspoons fresh ginger juice

Serves: 3

1. Reconstitute dried tofu by soaking it in lukewarm water 5 minutes. Repeatedly dampen and squeeze out excess water until liquid that comes out is no longer milky. Squeeze until fairly dry and dice.

2. Prepare Oriental marinade by combining listed ingredients in medium-sized bowl.

3. Toss tofu in marinade and let sit 30 minutes, tossing occasionally.

4. Heat oil in wok or large skillet, and sauté onion over medium-high heat until translucent.

5. Add carrots and pinch of salt. Sauté 1–2 minutes.

6. Add celery and 2–3 teaspoons of the marinade, and sauté 3–4 minutes.

7. Add green pepper and sauté 1–2 minutes.

8. Next, add mushrooms and small pinch of salt. Sauté 3 minutes.

9. Add tofu and marinade. Sauté a minute more.

10. Thoroughly dissolve kuzu in water or stock and add to pot while stirring briskly. Continue stirring a minute or two until broth thickens.

11. Serve immediately over freshly cooked udon or bifun noodles, millet, couscous, or rice.

12

UMEBOSHI

Venerable Pickled Plums

I n some Japanese cities it is not unusual to see a small, seventeenth-century, tile-roofed Buddhist temple nestled between tall, modern glass office buildings. Even in the more traditional countryside, the contrast between old and new can be stark. While one family sits at a contemporary Western-style dinner table eating juicy steak, their more typical neighbors are seated on the floor eating rice and miso soup with chopsticks.

However, when it comes to Japanese pickled plums, or *umeboshi* (literally, dried plum), everyone seems to agree that there is no modern substitute for its zesty palate-cleansing flavor and fast-acting medicinal effects. Even today, some traditional Japanese people begin the day with two pickled plums and a mug of tea. British author and Japanese food authority Robbie Swinnerton compares umeboshi's taste to the culinary equivalent of a cold shower. "The abrupt, searingly tart, tangy, salty taste jolts the eyes open, shakes the stomach awake, sandpapers off any staleness from the taste buds, and gets the day off to an unforgettable start." But besides their dramatic flavor, writes Swinnerton, "Japanese pickled plums have remarkable medicinal qualities. Their powerful acidity has a paradoxical alkalinizing effect on the body, neutralizing fatigue, stimulating the digestion, and promoting the elimination of toxins. This is the Far Eastern equivalent to both aspirin and apple; not only is it a potent hangover remedy for mornings after; more than that, an umeboshi a day is regarded as the best preventive medicine available."

Like many of Japan's ancient medicinal foods, the origin of the pickled plum is obscure. One theory traces it to China, where a dried smoked plum, or *ubai*, was discovered in a tomb built over two thousand years ago. The ubai is one of China's oldest medicines and is still used for a variety of medical purposes such as counteracting nausea, reducing fevers, and controlling coughs.

The oldest Japanese record of pickled plums being used as a medicine is in a medical text written about one thousand years ago. Umeboshi were used to prevent fatigue, purify water, rid the body of toxins, and cure specific diseases such as dysentery, typhoid, and food poisoning. Slowly, extensive folklore developed about umeboshi's ability to prevent and cure certain diseases.

During Japan's furious samurai period, which lasted through most of the Middle Ages, the pickled plum was the soldier's most important field ration. It was used to flavor foods such as rice and vegetables, and its high acidity made it an excellent water and food purifier, as well as an effective antidote for battle fatigue.

Today the Japanese make 15,000 tons of pickled plums annually. Although umeboshi is still considered an important food and medicine, its culinary and medicinal uses have branched into different products.

FOOD AND MEDICINE

As a food, pickled plums are usually used as a paste, a convenient red purée made from the flesh of pitted pickled plums. Another popular by-product of pickled plums is plum vinegar, or *ume su*, which is the red brine drawn from kegs of the mature pickled plums. More information about the use of whole pickled plums, paste, and plum vinegar appears in this chapter's cooking section, beginning on page 157.

Almost 200 years ago, the Japanese began experimenting with ways to concentrate the healing powers of umeboshi. Finally, a dark liquid called *bainiku ekisu* (plum extract) was developed. To make the extract, sour green umeboshi plums are slowly cooked down to obtain their most active ingredients in a highly concentrated form.

The resulting dark, sticky, thick liquid is usually mixed with hot water and honey and is drunk as a tonic. Dried plum extract is also formed into pills, called *meitan*. In both plum extract and meitan, the plums' citric acid content is concentrated tenfold, which is equivalent to about twenty-five times the content found in lemon juice.

Many natural healers around the world feel that these concentrated forms of Japanese plums are among the world's most effective natural medicines. Moreover, they do not have the high salt content of pickled plums.

The center of Japan's pickled-plum industry is in Wakayama Prefecture, on Japan's main island of Honshu. Even before the first orchards were planted, Wakayama's hillsides were abundant in wild plum trees. The area's mild temperatures, year-round plentiful rain, and sheltered geographic situation serve to bring forth the finest and most plentiful fruit in the country.

THE TRADITIONAL PROCESS

In the heart of Japan's pickled-plum region is Ryujin village, home of Yoshio Sogawa, one of Mitoku Company's pickled-plum manufacturers. Both Yoshio and his wife, Eriko, suffered from serious illnesses and cured themselves through eating a macrobiotic diet. Since that time, they have devoted their lives to practicing organic agriculture. Several years ago, the Sogawas began cultivating plum trees and now have an annual production of fifteen to twenty tons of Japan's finest pickled plums.

Using their own variation of the traditional methods used in Ryujin for centuries, the Sogawas make a mellow, tasty pickled plum that has less salt than typical Japanese pickled plums. The process used by the Sogawas is technically known as "lactic-acid fermentation," one of the oldest and safest ways of preserving food. Both desirable and undesirable bacteria are present when making umeboshi. "The secret to making good pickled plums," says Sogawa, "is getting lactic-acid-forming bacteria [the desirable type] to grow before other bacteria have a chance to multiply." While lactic-acid bacteria are salt-tolerant, many undesirable species are not. To help establish beneficial bacteria, traditional makers use the proper amount of salt, and store the fermenting plums in a cool, dark place. Lactic-acid bacteria multiply rapidly under these conditions. Once flourishing, they produce enough lactic acid and carbon dioxide to create an acidic environment that further inhibits the growth of undesirable microorganisms and enzymes. The carbon dioxide also contributes to a favorable anaerobic (low oxygen) condition and further stimulates the growth of lactic-acid bacteria.

At Ryujin, plums are picked around the end of June, when they are still green and their juice is at its peak of acidity. This guarantees the umeboshi to have as tart a taste as possible. "If they are picked too early," says Sogawa, "they are too hard, and their color never changes from green, but if left too long on the branch, the resulting pickles will be soft, mushy, and tasteless."

By the last week in June, the activity at Sogawa's shop is intense and non-stop from dawn to dusk. All the plums reach their full size at the same time and must be picked within a week or two. Any delay means the plums will begin to ripen, reducing their acidity, flavor, and medicinal qualities.

Next, the harvested plums are washed and then soaked overnight in water to remove any bitterness. The following day, the soaked plums are placed in large vats. A layer of jade green plums is topped with glistening white sea salt, followed by another layer, then another until each vat is filled with 5,500 pounds of plums and 638 pounds of salt. This brings the salt content to about 12 percent. In earlier times, before the link between strokes and salt consumption was clear, the salt content of pickled plums was over 25 percent!

The salt immediately begins to draw out the juice from the plums. A flat pressing lid topped with a heavy weight is placed on the plums to keep them submerged in the liquid. As the salt penetrates the flesh of the fruit, the pickling process begins; the plums are left to ferment until the end of July (the end of the rainy season). Taken from the vats, the pickled plums are placed on wooden racks and left outside to dry for anywhere from four to seven days, depending on the weather.

Although the pickling process is now complete, the wrinkled and shriveled plums do not have the dramatic red color and aromatic flavor of Sogawa's prized organic pickled plums. To make these finest umeboshi, he must soak the plums in plum vinegar along with leaves of the beautiful, scented shiso *(perilla)* plant.

An herb that is related to mint, shiso has a slight lemony taste yet a unique flavor of its own. Its red, heart-shaped leaves are reminiscent of red meat, hence comes one of its English names, "beefsteak plant." Besides adding color and flavor to umeboshi, shiso has strong antibacterial and preservative qualities both in the pickling process and on the person who eats them. It is this that makes shiso such a perfect garnish in the sushi shop.

To add the essence of shiso leaves to his pickled plums, Sogawa mixes the leaves with the liquid (vinegar) that is left from the pickling process. The shiso leaves turn the liquid a brilliant red, and the umeboshi are left to steep in this liquid for five days. When the plums are removed from the plum vinegar, they are placed in vats and left to age for up to one year. The remaining red liquid is bottled and sold as tangy plum vinegar.

SHOPPING FOR UMEBOSHI

Although there are many natural producers of pickled plums in Japan, few use the year-long traditional process of Mitoku's two suppliers: the Sogawa family and the Morimoto family of the Morisho Company. Fewer still use organically grown plums and high-quality sea salt. In fact, the umeboshi found in many Oriental foods stores are made in just a few weeks using red dye, organic acids, and commercial salt. To be sure that you are buying the finest-quality pickled plums, check the ingredients on the label. Sogawa-style pickled plums are made with organic plums, organic shiso leaves, and sea salt.

In less than a decade, the worldwide demand for the Sogawa family's pickled plums, paste, and vinegar has outgrown their tiny orchard. Recently, the Sogawas have been teaching the traditional method and organic agriculture to neighboring plum farmers. Their commitment to the labor-intense, ancient plum-pickling process and natural agriculture is keeping this way of life alive in the mountains surrounding Ryujin village. Look for Sogawa's organic umeboshi under the Mitoku Macrobiotic and Kaiseki Select labels. Marisho's products are available under the Emperor's Kitchen and Kaiseki Select labels.

COOKING WITH UMEBOSHI, UMEBOSHI PASTE, AND PLUM VINEGAR

Umeboshi and umeboshi paste are lively and versatile seasonings that add a pleasant tartness to salad dressings, cooked vegetables, and sauces. Umeboshi is also commonly served in Japan as a condiment with rice, or tucked inside a rice ball wrapped with nori. In the summer, thick cucumber rounds spread thinly with umeboshi paste are a cooling treat. Sparingly spread on cooked sweet corn, it is a delicious, healthful alternative to butter and salt. Umeboshi also goes well with members of the cabbage family, including broccoli, kale, and cauliflower.

When using whole pickled plums, it is usually necessary to remove the pit and mince the flesh before adding it to recipes. Umeboshi paste can be substituted for umeboshi in virtually any recipe.

The shiso leaves that are often packaged with umeboshi are also delicious when chopped and used as a seasoning inside nori rolls or when tossed in with steamed or sautéed vegetables.

Plum vinegar contains many of the healing qualities and nutrients associated with pickled plums, and it is easy and convenient to use. Both pleasantly tart and salty, plum vinegar is a versatile seasoning that is especially refreshing on hot afternoons. Use pickled plum vinegar to liven up salad dressings, homemade quick pickles, and tofu spreads. It adds a pleasantly pungent flavor to cooked leafy greens (especially cabbage), cauliflower, broccoli, and green beans.

Steam, boil, or sauté vegetables until tender but still colorful. Drain if necessary, place in a serving bowl, and toss with plum vinegar to taste. When substituting plum vinegar for other types of vinegar, substantially reduce the amount used, or eliminate the salt in the recipe. The following recipes will help you become familiar with umeboshi and plum vinegar and will soon have you discovering new ways to use these delicious and healthful seasonings.

Umeboshi plums drying in the sun.

UMEBOSHI RECIPES

Braised Cabbage With Umeboshi

Umeboshi goes particularly well with vegetables in the cabbage family and with daikon radish.

$1/2$ head medium-sized cabbage

2 teaspoons sesame oil

1 tablespoon plus 1 teaspoon umeboshi paste or minced umeboshi

Serves: 3

1. Cut the cabbage half in half again lengthwise. Remove and thinly slice the core. Cut cabbage quarters crosswise into $1/8$–$1/4$-inch slices.

2. Heat oil in a skillet, add umeboshi, and sauté briefly.

3. Add cabbage and toss with umeboshi. (At first, umeboshi will not disperse evenly, but as you continue tossing and sautéeing, it will evenly coat cabbage.)

4. After sautéeing, if no juice has come out of the cabbage, add a little water, cover, and simmer over low heat until tender (15–20 minutes).

5. Serve hot.

Orange-Ume Dressing

This is a refreshing summer dressing for tossed salads and noodle salads.

3 level tablespoons toasted sesame seeds or 3 tablespoons tahini
2 teaspoons umeboshi paste or minced umeboshi
2 tablespoons light sesame or olive oil
1 tablespoon lemon juice
Juice of 1–1 ½ oranges (to taste)
1 teaspoon minced scallion or chives (optional)

Yield: 1 cup

1. Toast sesame seeds (if using) in a dry skillet over medium heat for 1–2 minutes, stirring constantly. When seeds are fragrant and begin to pop, remove from pan to prevent them from overcooking and becoming bitter.

2. Blend first 5 ingredients in a blender until smooth.

3. Mix in scallions or chives (if desired), and chill for 30 minutes before using.

▲ To produce high-quality Johsen shoyu, shoyu moromi is gently stirred every day for eighteen months at the Sendai Shoyu and Miso Company.

▲ Junzo Oguri, president of Mansan Brewing Company, performs the daily task of mixing tamari moromi.

▲ Workers hand-pick tea leaves
at the Nagata plantation.

▶ Umeboshi plums dry in
the sun.

▲ With active Japanese volcano Mt. Sakurajima in the distance, workers at the Maruboshi Vinegar Company pour rice vinegar ingredients into earthenware crocks to ferment.

▲ Kanten, a sea-vegetable "gelatin," naturally freeze-dries in the winter sun.

◀ *Haru Arai, one of Japan's last traditional barrel makers (okeyasan) splits a bamboo shaft.*

▶ *Arai completes the final stages of braiding a bamboo hoop.*

Cole Slaw

This salad goes well with almost any natural-foods entrée. Toasted sunflower seeds add concentrated nutrition and extra flavor.

$^1\!/_2$ small head cabbage
$^1\!/_2$ teaspoon sea salt
1 large carrot, finely grated (peel if not organic)
$^1\!/_3$ cup Nayonnaise*
2 teaspoons plum vinegar
1 $^1\!/_2$ teaspoons brown rice vinegar or lemon juice
1 teaspoon rice syrup
$^1\!/_4$ cup sunflower seeds

Serves: 4

1. Cut the cabbage half in half again lengthwise. Remove tough core and reserve for another use. Slice cabbage crosswise, as thinly as possible.

2. Rinse cabbage and drain well (shake to remove excess water), then place in a large bowl. Add salt, toss well, and knead (squeeze handfuls to help soften fibers). Set aside at least 20 minutes, then squeeze out excess water.

3. Add carrot to cabbage and toss until evenly mixed.

4. Make dressing by combining Nayonnaise, plum vinegar, brown rice vinegar or lemon juice, and rice syrup. Add dressing to vegetables and toss well.

5. Toast sunflower seeds in a dry skillet over medium heat, stirring constantly until golden and fragrant. Transfer to a small bowl.

6. If time permits, chill cole slaw slightly in refrigerator.

7. Top with sprinkling of seeds. Serve remaining seeds on the side to be added to individual servings, as desired.

---

*A tofu-based substitute for mayonnaise that is widely available in natural foods stores. Of course, natural mayonnaise can be substituted in this recipe.

Umeboshi Tea

Umeboshi tea, taken warm, helps combat fatigue, improve circulation, and aid digestion.

1 cup kukicha tea (see page 139)
½ large or 1 small umeboshi, pitted and shredded
A few drops shoyu (to taste)
A few drops fresh ginger juice

Yield: 1 cup

1. Bring kukicha tea to a boil. Remove from heat, add umeboshi, shoyu, and ginger juice.

2. Let steep 1–2 minutes before drinking.

13

VEGETABLES OF THE SEA
Underwater Harvest

Harvesting plants from the sea may be the wave of the future, but many varieties of sea vegetables have been enjoyed since before the development of agriculture. Properly prepared, high-quality sea vegetables are delicious and provide a concentrated source of nutrition.

Sea vegetables are virtually fat-free; low in calories; and rich in essential minerals, vitamins, protein, and important trace elements that are often lacking in land vegetables due to soil demineralization. "Sea vegetables contain more minerals than any other kind of food," claim Doctors Seibin and Teruko Arasaki, authors of *Vegetables From the Sea*. Analysis has shown that a wide range of minerals account for 7–38 percent of their dry weight. All of the elements essential to health—including calcium, sodium, magnesium, potassium, iodine, iron, and zinc—are present in sea vegetables in sufficient amounts. Of the wide variety of minerals present, calcium, iron, and iodine are of particular importance to people eating a dairy-free, grain-based vegetarian, or macrobiotic diet. For example, $\frac{1}{4}$ cup of cooked hijiki contains over half the calcium found in a cup of milk and more iron than in an egg. Although iodine is, by nature, volatile and somewhat difficult to obtain, sea vegetables contain complex natural sugars that stabilize their iodine, making them excellent sources of this essential mineral.

Edible plants from the sea also contain important vitamins including vitamin A (in the form of beta-carotene), B_1, B_2, B_6, niacin, vitamin C, pantothenic acid, and folic acid. Analysis has shown trace amounts of vitamin B_{12}, which rarely occurs in land vegetables.

For those watching their weight, sea vegetables are the perfect food. Their carbohydrates pass through the digestive system as complex fiber, cleansing the intestines while adding no calories to the diet.

Besides their impressive nutritional profile, sea vegetables offer other health benefits. For centuries, Oriental medicine has recognized that sea vegetables contribute to general well-being and especially to the health of the endocrine and nervous systems. Over the last few decades, medical researchers have discovered a diet that includes sea vegetables reduces the risk of some diseases and helps the body eliminate dangerous toxins. In fact, surveys show that people living in areas where sea vegetables are regularly included in the diet tend to live longer, healthier lives (see *Medicine From the Sea*, page 167).

One reason sea vegetables are so nutritious is due to the ideal growing conditions of the world's oceans. Living in a marine environment, sea vegetables have ready access to the abundance of nutrients found in the ocean. The gentle wave action of the underwater currents delivers nutrients to sea vegetables and carries away the plants' waste. As a result, sea vegetables concentrate minerals and other nutrients at levels that are rarely found in land plants.

Although biologists classify sea vegetables as plants, the only important characteristic they share with typical land plants is the ability to make food (sugar) from sunlight, carbon dioxide, and water. Both sea and land plants use a light-activated catalytic chemical reaction to accomplish this. In green sea vegetables, like land plants, the catalyst is the green pigment chlorophyll. In red and brown sea vegetables, other pigments predominate.

One way scientists classify sea vegetables is by their color. Most of the popular edible sea vegetables, such as wakame, kombu, arame, and hijiki are classified as brown sea vegetables (algae) while nori—the most widely used sea vegetable—falls under the classification of red sea vegetables. Scientists believe that the different colored pigments allow sea vegetables to make food in the ocean depths, where light intensity and wave lengths are different from those found at the surface.

Beyond the ability to make food, sea vegetables bear little resemblance to land plants. Since they have no true leaves, stems, or roots, and as they reproduce by a primitive method that does not utilize flowers or seeds, sea vegetables are structurally more like mushrooms and other fungi. From a chef's point of view, the simple structure of sea vegetables is an asset. Without woody roots and stems, there is much more to eat.

Like land vegetables, the quality of sea vegetables can vary. In Japan, most sea vegetables are supplied in bulk by brokers or middlemen who buy from growers or harvesters in large quantities. The bulk sea vegetables are then packaged under various Oriental and natural foods labels. Some sea vegetables are now artificially cultivated and others are picked from or grown in polluted waters. However, the highest quality sea vegetables are picked wild from clean waters at just the right time. Mitoku Macrobiotic sea vegetables are bought from the small traditional suppliers described on the following pages, who have been harvesting wild sea vegetables as a way of life for decades.

Medicine From the Sea

For thousands of years, herbalists and pharmacologists around the world have tested and experimented with medicinal plants. Many modern medicines are either derived from plant extracts or are synthetic copies of substances originally derived from plants. Although there is a long tradition of using sea vegetables as medicine in Japan and China, modern medicine usually regards these remedies as mere folklore.

More recent medicinal treatments using sea vegetables, sea water, and mud from the ocean—such as thalassotherapy and algotherapy—are primarily external applications rather than internal medicines. Advocates of these therapies claim reduced or cured symptoms of hypertension, chronic rheumatism, gout, neuralgia, asthma, eczema, and even hemorrhoids.

Current interest in the medicinal value of sea vegetables began in 1927, when Professor S. Kondo, of Tohoku University, discovered that Japanese people living in regions where large amounts of sea vegetables were eaten regularly enjoyed a particularly long lifespan. For example, on Oki Island in the Shimane prefecture, where people eat an abundance of sea vegetables, there is the longest life expectancy in the nation. Before World War II, it was not uncommon to see Oki women who were 70 years old and older diving in the sea for abalone and red algae.

Since Kondo's field work, scientists have discovered that sea vegetables, in addition to being very nutritious, have antibiotic and anti-tumor properties. Sea vegetables have also been found to reduce blood pressure and serum cholesterol.

As a result of this research, a few new medicines have been developed from this underwater harvest, such as laminin, which is used to reduce blood pressure. The most important discovery about sea vegetables for modern living, however, is their ability to cleanse the body of toxins. This powerful cleansing action has been linked to a substance called alginic acid.

Alginic acid is a polysaccharide that is abundant in those sea vegetables classified as brown algae, including kombu, hijiki, arame, and wakame. Scientific researchers, including a team led by Dr. Tanaka at McGill University, have demonstrated that alginic acid binds with any heavy metals found in the intestines, renders them indigestible, and causes them to be eliminated. So, any heavy metals, such as barium, cadmium, lead, mercury, zinc, and even radioactive strontium, that may be present in the intestines will not be absorbed by the body when alginic acid is present.

Doctors Seibin and Teruko Arasaki, Japanese scientists who have published several books about sea vegetables, also report this cleansing property of alginic acid in their book *Vegetables From the Sea*. They conclude, "Heavy metals taken into the human body are rendered insoluble by alginic acid in the intestines and cannot, therefore, be absorbed into body tissues."

What's more, Dr. Tanaka's research has shown that the alginic acid in sea vegetables actually helps bind and draw out any similar toxins that are already stored in our bodies, thus "lowering the body's burden."

KOMBU

In the cold seas off Hokkaido, Japan's northernmost island, a brown algae known as kombu or kelp, grows in a dense underwater forest. Swaying with the rhythm of the sea, individual fronds reach up from the ocean floor sometimes to a height of over thirty feet.

Of the many different grades of kombu gathered from Japan's clear arctic waters, those from Hidaka province are prized above all others. By late summer, the kombu is ready to harvest. Floating on the water in small skiffs, men and women cut the kombu free using razor-sharp knives that are attached to long bamboo poles. As the kombu floats to the surface it is gathered with wooden rakes and placed in the boats. Once back on land, the kombu is laid out to dry slowly and naturally in the sun.

The quality of Hidaka kombu is evident from its broad flat blade, and its deep, even color when soaked and reconstituted. The white minerals found on the kombu's dried surface contain the prized natural glutamic salts that help make kombu a supreme flavoring agent. These minerals should not be washed off. Simply wipe the kombu with a damp cloth before use.

COOKING WITH KOMBU

Kombu can be used to create delicious clear soups and cooling pressed salads, as well as hearty stews and bean dishes. In most recipes kombu need not be soaked before use. When soaking is called for, merely soak the kombu until it softens and opens up. The nutritious soaking water can be used in the recipe, or reserved and used at a later time in soups or stews.

Kombu's most common and important use is in the preparation of dashi, Japan's multipurpose stock for soups, stews, and sauces. Dashi appears simple, but it is integral to Japanese cooking, since it is the first step in many traditional dishes. The flavor and quality of the stock help determine the taste of the finished dish. The traditional method for making dashi is given on page 105.

Kombu is also good when sliced and used in soups, stews, and vegetable and bean dishes. When cooking beans, the addition of kombu is particularly recommended because it helps soften the beans, reduces cooking time, and makes them easier to digest. The Japanese commonly use kombu to enhance the flavor of the brine or "mash" that is used to marinate various types of pickles. Sometimes, the kombu itself is one of the ingredients to be pickled. Kombu can also be cooked in a seasoned broth, wrapped around pieces of burdock or other vegetables, and then served as hors d'oeuvres.

A nutritious condiment can be made by roasting kombu then grinding it to a powder. First, cut the kombu into small pieces and place in an unoiled skillet over medium heat. Stir the kombu pieces constantly until they become very crisp. Transfer the roasted kombu pieces into a bowl or a suribachi (Japanese grinding bowl), and grind the kombu into a fine powder. Add this powder as a seasoning to soups, or sprinkle it over grains and vegetable dishes before serving.

Kombu Stock

This subtle, flavor-enhancing stock can be made in a very short time using only kombu and water. Simply combine 4–6 cups of water and a 6-inch piece of dried kombu in a saucepan. Bring just to a simmer, uncovered, over medium heat, then immediately remove kombu. This technique gives the most delicate and delicious results.

Another stock-making method is to put a 6-inch piece of kombu in 4–6 cups of water, and let it soak one or two hours. Make sure to reserve the kombu—it can be cooked with beans or vegetables, or reused one or two times for making more stock.

If reusing the kombu to make stock, bring water to a boil, add kombu, then reduce heat and simmer 10–20 minutes. Lightly scoring the kombu will help release the amino acid responsible for its flavor-intensifying effect. For a more flavorful variation, see Dashi (page 105).

KOMBU RECIPES

Hearty Baked Vegetables

This warming dish, with its attractive fall colors, is especially appealing during autumn or winter.

6-inch strip kombu

1 cup water

1 large onion, halved and sliced into wedges

$\frac{1}{2}$ head cabbage, sliced into $\frac{3}{4}$-inch wedges

2–3 large carrots, cut into small bite-sized chunks

$\frac{1}{2}$ butternut squash (peeled) or buttercup squash (unpeeled),
cut into large bite-sized chunks

1 tablespoon plus 1 teaspoon shoyu

Serves: 3–4

1. Preheat oven to 375°F. Place kombu in a pie plate or small baking dish. Add water and soak at least 10 minutes. Remove kombu and cut it into 1-inch pieces, reserving soaking water.

2. Place all vegetables in a baking pan or casserole dish. Add shoyu to kombu soaking water and pour over vegetables. Cover and bake until tender (about 50–60 minutes).

3. Serve hot.

Kombu Shoyu Pickles*

Here's a tasty variation on a popular Japanese pickle.

$^1\!/_2$ *cup shoyu*
1 cup water
6-inch strip kombu, cut into 1-inch pieces
1 $^1\!/_2$ cups thinly sliced turnips
5 thin slices peeled fresh ginger root

Yield: 1 $^1\!/_2$ cups

1. Sterilize a pint-sized jar by boiling it in water for 10 minutes. Remove and drain.

2. Combine all ingredients, place in jar, and cover with cheesecloth. Keep in a cool place for 3 days.

3. Remove cheesecloth, cover jar tightly with a cap, and let stand 2 more days before eating.

4. Store in a refrigerator or cold place and use within one month.

*Recipe from Peter and Montse Bradford, authors of *Cooking With Sea Vegetables*.

HIJIKI

It has been said that the thick, black, lustrous hair of the Japanese is partly due to their regular diet of hijiki, a brown sea algae. Indeed, this black cylindrical sea vegetable resembles hair as it grows on the ocean floor. Research has shown that minerals are important to healthy hair growth, and hijiki has an incredible 34 grams of minerals per every 100 grams. In fact, there is more calcium in hijiki than that contained in an equal weight of cow's milk. So, there is probably some truth to this Japanese old wive's tale.

Boshu hijiki, which is harvested along the Boshu peninsula on the east coast of Japan's main island, is Japan's premium hijiki. The mild climate of Boshu is ideal for this sea vegetable, which flourishes along the rocky tideline.

Once fishermen, the Nishikawa family now specializes in the gathering and preparation of Boshu hijiki according to traditional methods. This vegetable from the sea is harvested in the early spring, just as it reaches its peak of flavor. When the lowest tides expose the shallows, the hijiki is cut and brought into the Nishikawa shop. After it is washed, the entire plant is steamed for nine hours in its own juices. At this point, the plant has softened considerably, and its color has changed from light brown to black. Left overnight to cool, it is then thoroughly air-dried before being packaged.

The traditional process used by the Nishikawas differs from the methods that are typically used to prepare commercial hijiki. In the commercial process, hijiki is boiled in water for long periods, resulting in mineral loss. It is also common for commercial hijiki harvesters to damage plants, leaving behind important structures that are high in nutrients. Boshu hijiki is carefully selected and contains both stems and buds of the plant; because of this, it is known as "whole" hijiki. Look for Boshu whole hijiki under the Mitoku Macrobiotic label.

ARAME

Like hijiki, arame is a brown algae, but it grows in deeper waters and has a much milder taste. Much of Japan's arame is gathered off the Ise peninsula, the site of one of Japan's most famous shrines.

In late summer, local fishermen wade out to gather the young, tender plants at low tide, or dive into shallow waters and cut the arame from its holdfast. The plants are then finely shredded and processed in a manner similar to that of hijiki.

COOKING WITH HIJIKI AND ARAME

When properly cooked and presented, hijiki is very attractive. Its shimmering black color adds vivid contrast and beauty to any meal. When planning a meal that includes hijiki, try to use foods with colors that create an attractive contrast to the blackness of the hijiki. Carrots, winter squash, and pumpkin offer deep orange colors, while lightly steamed broccoli and watercress provide bright green tones. Cold hijiki salad topped with a creamy white tofu dressing and a sprinkle of finely minced green onion or parsley presents an attractive contrast of colors, and is particularly appealing on a hot summer day.

Although hijiki and arame are prepared in similar ways, there are a few important differences. Hijiki is thicker, somewhat coarser, and has a strong ocean flavor. Arame's considerably milder aroma and taste make it a good choice for anyone just beginning to use sea vegetables.

Both should be rinsed quickly but carefully to remove foreign matter such as sand and shells, then soaked in water to cover. However, because of the difference in their textures, hijiki should be soaked for ten minutes, while the more delicate arame needs only five. Longer soaking draws out the important nutrients and waterlogs these vegetables making them less able to absorb the flavor of seasonings used in the recipe.

If you use the soaking water in cooking, pour it carefully so as not to disturb any sand or shells that have sunk to the bottom. Keep back a small amount in the bowl and then discard it. Using the soaking water results in a somewhat stronger flavor and decreases the need for added salt or shoyu. In the recipes that follow, fresh water was used, so if you choose to use soaking water, cut the amount of shoyu in half, and add more only if needed.

Take into consideration that soaking increases the dried volume of arame and hijiki by about three times. One cup of dried hijiki will become three cups when soaked. For general preparation, squeeze out excess water after soaking and sauté the sea vegetable in a little oil for a few minutes. Add soaking water or fresh water to almost cover and simmer until the vegetable is tender and most of the liquid is absorbed (about thirty-five minutes for hijiki and twenty-five minutes for arame). Finally, season the tender vegetables with shoyu and mirin (if desired), and cook a few minutes more.

Both hijiki and arame are delicious when sautéed with sweet vegetables such as carrots, slow-cooked onions, winter squash, lotus root, shiitake, and dried daikon radish. Hijiki and arame are also delicious when served with deep-fried fresh tofu or when sautéed with dried tofu. A little chopped hijiki or arame can be combined with cooked rice, millet, or barley. Hijiki and arame are good additions to salads, especially when topped with a tofu dressing.

HIJIKI/ARAME RECIPES

Although the following recipes are for hijiki, if you wish to use arame, simply make the previously-mentioned adjustments in soaking and cooking time (page 174).

Hijiki Summer Salad*

This salad is a wonderful way to get mineral-rich hijiki into your diet.

$\frac{1}{2}$ *cup dried hijiki*
Water to cover hijiki
1 tablespoon shoyu
Pinch sea salt
3 ears fresh corn
$\frac{1}{2}$ *cup shelled green peas*
$\frac{1}{2}$ *cup bean sprouts*
$\frac{1}{2}$ *cup grated carrots*

DRESSING
4 tablespoons natural prepared mustard
2 tablespoons sesame butter or tahini
3 tablespoons brown rice vinegar
$\frac{1}{2}$ *cup water*

Serves: 4–6

1. Soak hijiki 10 minutes. Drain, reserving soaking water, and rinse hijiki in a colander. Slice into 1$\frac{1}{2}$-inch lengths.

2. Slowly pour soaking water into a pot (discarding any sediment). Add hijiki and, if necessary, fresh water to almost cover. Bring to a boil, cover, reduce heat, and simmer 35 minutes.

3. Add shoyu and cook until water has evaporated (approximately 10 minutes). Remove from heat and set aside.

4. Bring another pot of water to a boil, add pinch of salt and corn cobs. Simmer 15 minutes. Take corn from water, allow to cool, then remove kernels from cobs.

5. In the same water, boil the peas 10 minutes, and then the bean sprouts 1 minute. Place on a plate to cool after cooking.

6. In a serving bowl, mix hijiki, corn, peas, bean sprouts, and raw carrot.

7. Blend dressing ingredients together until smooth, then add dressing to salad. Mix well before serving.

---

*Recipe from Peter and Montse Bradford, authors of *Cooking With Sea Vegetables*.

Hijiki With Snow-Dried Tofu and Vegetables

This colorful combination of hijiki, carrots, and parsley is delicious and appealing. Dried tofu supplies additional concentrated nutrition and an interesting texture. Mirin lightens the flavor and provides a mild sweetness.

1 ¼ cups (1.76-ounce package) dried hijiki
Water to cover hijiki
2 teaspoons sesame oil
4 pieces snow-dried tofu
1 ½-2 tablespoons natural soy sauce (to taste)
1 tablespoon mirin
1 carrot, cut into julienne strips
2-3 tablespoons minced parsley

Serves: 6-8

1. In a bowl, place hijiki and water to cover. Let soak 10 minutes.

2. Drain and briefly rinse hijiki to remove any sand and shells.

3. Heat oil in a large skillet, add hijiki, and sauté 1-2 minutes. Add fresh water to almost cover and bring to a boil. Lower heat, cover, and simmer.

4. Reconstitute dried tofu by soaking it in lukewarm water for 5 minutes. Repeatedly dampen and squeeze out excess water until the liquid that comes out is no longer milky. Dice tofu, add to skillet, and toss. Simmer for 25 minutes.

5. Add soy sauce and mirin, and toss together with hijiki and tofu.

6. Place carrots on top of hijiki mixture, cover, and let cook 10 minutes more. Toss. If any liquid remains, cook uncovered over high heat a few minutes until nearly dry.

7. Sprinkle parsley on top, cover, and steam 1 minute.

8. Serve hot.

Arame With Deep-Fried Tofu*

Fried tofu and arame make a delicious combination. The addition of watercress offers fresh taste and eye appeal.

8-ounce block tofu

3 tablespoons arrowroot

Sesame or other light vegetable oil for deep frying

1 cup dried arame

Water to cover arame

1 tablespoon mirin

½ tablespoon shoyu

2 bunches watercress, cut into 1-inch lengths

Serves: 3

1. To remove excess moisture, wrap tofu in a clean, dry kitchen towel and place on a wooden cutting board. Place a 2–3 pound weight on top and leave 20–30 minutes. Uncover tofu, cut crosswise into ½-inch slices, then cut slices into ¾-inch cubes.

2. Roll tofu cubes in arrowroot to lightly coat all surfaces.

3. In a small, deep pot, heat 2 inches oil to 350°F. Add several pieces of tofu (do not overcrowd pot) and fry until golden brown. (Remove all pieces from one batch before adding more tofu.) Drain fried tofu on absorbent paper towel.

4. Rinse arame quickly under cold water and soak 5–7 minutes. Drain, reserving soaking water, and rinse again.

5. Place arame in a pot and add soaking water (discarding any sediment). If needed, add fresh water to almost cover arame. Bring to a boil.

6. Add mirin. Cover pot, reduce heat, and simmer 15 minutes.

7. Add shoyu and fried tofu. Cook until most liquid has evaporated (about 10 minutes).

8. Add watercress and mix well.

9. Place in a bowl and serve.

---

*Recipe from Peter and Montse Bradford, authors of *Cooking With Sea Vegetables*.

NORI

Japanese nori is a sea vegetable that has been dried and pressed into thin sheets. Versatile and easy to prepare, nori is rich in protein and in vitamins A, B, and C; it is also abundant in a wide range of nutrients, most notably calcium and iron. Presently, the Japanese consume almost 9 billion sheets of nori per year. Nori is also quickly gaining worldwide popularity, due partly to the proliferation of successful sushi bars that offer various combinations of rice and vegetables or fish wrapped in nori.

Along the northeast coast of Japan, in the Sendai region, are the pine-covered islands of scenic Matsushima. This pure, cold-water coastline is a seemingly endless series of quiet coves and sheltered shallows—the perfect place to grow nori seaweed.

Although originally gathered wild, nori has been cultivated by the Japanese for over 300 years. Nets made of woven rope are suspended between long bamboo poles that are set deep into the gentle bays. During the cold months of winter, the nori slowly grows until it covers the entire net. The nets are positioned so they remain above the water level during low tide in order for the growing nori to get maximum sunlight, yet receive a regular washing below the water level during high tide. In January and February, this fragile, green seaweed is gathered from the water by hand and brought ashore. There the nori is washed, first in sea water, then in fresh water; it is finally placed in bamboo frames to dry slowly and carefully, a process much like the making of fine paper.

Like many foods in Japan, nori is available in numerous grades. Mitoku Macrobiotic Sendai Select has been chosen from the top 1 percent of all Japanese nori. Its fine, even texture and translucent, deep-green color are indications of its high quality. Lesser grades of nori are a dull, purplish-black and lack Sendai nori's vibrant luster. When nori quality is important, such as when making fine sushi, Sendai nori is often the choice.

COOKING WITH NORI

Except for "sushi nori," which comes pretoasted, just before using, nori should be lightly toasted by briefly passing the unfolded sheet over a gas flame or electric burner. The nori is ready when the color changes to a more brilliant green and it becomes crisp and fragrant. (Be careful when toasting—nori is delicate and burns easily.)

Nori is most commonly used to wrap around rice balls, which are probably the most common and popular addition to Japanese lunchboxes and picnic baskets. Nori is also used to wrap other foods, such as *Nori-Maki* (page 182). Cut into 2-inch strips, nori is delicious when wrapped around mouthfuls of warm rice dabbed with umeboshi paste. Crumbled or cut into strips, nori can be used to garnish soups, vegetables, and grain or noodle dishes.

Recently nori is being used as a party food in a variation of nori-maki called *te-maki*. Te-maki literally means "wrapping by hand." A quarter sheet of toasted nori is topped with a little sushi rice or noodles along with an assortment of foods such as raw tuna, avocado, or raw vegetables. Condiments such as umeboshi or wasabi can be added, then the nori "package" is rolled into a funnel or cone shape. Te-maki adds an exotic flair to parties, especially when served with hot sake.

Another variety of nori, called *aonori*, or green nori, is sold in flake form. Aonori is used as a garnish or as a seasoning in fried rice. This type of nori is the richest in iron and protein.

NORI RECIPES

Stuffed Nori Cones*

Also called te-maki, these cones make an attractive snack, party food, or meal starter.

2 sheets toasted nori
(see Cooking with Nori, page 179)
1 cup cooked brown rice
$\frac{1}{2}$ cup chopped watercress
$\frac{1}{2}$ cup grated carrots
4 tablespoons toasted sesame seeds
1 tablespoon lemon juice
1 tablespoon natural prepared mustard
1 tablespoon umeboshi vinegar
Watercress sprigs for garnish

Yield: 8 cones

1. With scissors, cut each nori sheet in half lengthwise, then cut both pieces in half crosswise to make four quarters. Set aside.

2. Place all remaining ingredients in a bowl and mix together well.

3. Taking one piece of nori at a time, carefully fold into a cone shape. A drop of water will cause overlapping sides to stick.

4. Just before serving, fill each cone with the mix, decorating the top of each with a sprig of watercress.

5. Arrange filled cones neatly on a tray and serve.

*Recipe from Peter and Montse Bradford, authors of *Cooking With Sea Vegetables*.

Nori Maki (Sushi Nori Rolls)*

There is a knack to making good sushi that can be learned easily with a little practice. The key is the quality of the cooked rice, which should be slightly sticky and freshly cooked; it should be fairly cool but still contain some warmth. Take time to spread the rice evenly over the nori and to position the filling ingredients carefully. Roll up the nori slowly so the filling does not spill out.

Sesame or other light vegetable oil for deep frying
$\frac{1}{2}$ *cup seitan (wheat meat) pieces*
2 sheets toasted nori
(see Cooking with Nori, *page 179*)
3 cups cooked brown rice, slightly cooled
2 tablespoons natural prepared mustard
$\frac{1}{2}$ *teaspoon shoyu*

Yield: 2 rolls (12–16 bite-sized pieces)

1. In a small, deep pot, heat 2 inches oil to 350°F.

2. Squeeze excess liquid from seitan and deep-fry until slightly brown and crisp (about 2 minutes). Remove and drain on absorbent paper. When cool enough to handle, cut seitan into thin strips.

3. Place one nori sheet on a bamboo sushi mat with the stripping of the mat running from left to right. Spread half the cooked brown rice evenly over the nori, leaving a clear $\frac{1}{2}$-inch space at bottom of the mat and 1 inch at the top.

4. With a chopstick, make an indentation in the center of rice running from left to right.

5. Mix mustard and shoyu together, and spread half of mixture evenly over rice.

6. Place half of seitan strips in indentation across rice.

7. Starting at the bottom, roll up the sushi mat around the ingredients, pressing the mat firmly onto the nori. While rolling, slowly pull the leading edge of

the mat back so it does not roll into the sushi. Continue rolling until the uncovered end of the nori is reached. Dampen this edge slightly with water and complete rolling to seal the sushi. A final gentle squeeze of the mat around the sushi will ensure a tight roll.

8. Prepare the second roll.

9. With a sharp knife, slice each roll in half, and then cut each half into 3 or 4 rounds. (To prevent sushi from drying out, cut just before serving.)

10. Arrange, cut side up, on platter or individual plates, and serve.

---

*Recipe from Peter and Montse Bradford, authors of *Cooking With Sea Vegetables*.

WAKAME

The artificial cultivation of wakame, a brown algae related to kombu, is a growing industry in Japan. A technical understanding of wakame's complex life cycle has enabled businessmen to grow young wakame in tanks and then transplant them to the ocean floor once they are mature enough to fend for themselves. The mature plants are then harvested by machine and dried by hot air.

Although rare, some wild wakame, such as Mitoku's premium San-Riku Sun-Dried Wild Wakame, is still harvested in Japan. The remote fishing villages on the San-Riku coast of northeastern Japan are renowned for superb seafood. The cold Pacific waters are clean and clear, providing the perfect environment for wakame. The wild wakame from San-Riku has a vitality and depth of flavor that is unequaled by cultivated varieties. There is no "fishy" taste, and the fronds are particularly tender and tasty.

Around San-Riku, the wakame harvest takes place in early spring, from February until the end of March, as the plants reach maximum size, and before their leaves start to harden. The local fishermen go out in small boats and cut the seaweed by hand, using long, razor-sharp sickles to cut the stems. The wakame is brought back to land, briefly washed, then hung up to dry in the sun for several days until it is completely crisp and dry.

COOKING WITH WAKAME

The taste and texture of different varieties of wakame vary considerably. If you have been put off by the strong ocean flavor and relatively tough texture of one brand, look for a wild variety. You may be surprised at how mild and delicious wakame can be.

Dried wakame is reconstituted by soaking in water for ten to fifteen minutes. Once soaked, remove the wakame, squeeze out the excess moisture, cut away any tough ribs, and slice. Wakame is especially good in soups and salads. It can also be added to stews and vegetable or bean dishes. Wakame is tender and should not be cooked for more than a few minutes.

A nutritious condiment can be made by toasting dried wakame (be careful—it burns easily) over a flame in a dry skillet or in the oven. Once toasted, the wakame is crumbled or ground into a powder. Toasted sesame seeds may be added and ground with the toasted wakame. This condiment can be sprinkled over grains, tossed with cooked rice, or added as a seasoning to soups and salads.

WAKAME RECIPES

Wakame Miso Soup

This is an energizing way to start the day, and our favorite way to enjoy wakame.

6 cups Kombu Stock *(page 170)* or Dashi *(page 105)*
1 medium carrot, cut in half lengthwise and thinly sliced on the diagonal
6-inch section wakame
2 scallions, thinly sliced on the diagonal
3–4 tablespoons red (rice) or barley miso,
or combination of 2 tablespoons dark miso and
2–3 tablespoons mellow white miso

Serves: 4

1. In a medium-sized pot, bring stock to a simmer. Add carrots and simmer until tender (10–15 minutes).

2. Soak wakame in cold or tepid water for 10 minutes, cut away any tough ribs, and slice fronds into 1-inch pieces.

3. When carrots are tender, add wakame to soup, and simmer 1 minute. Add scallions and simmer another minute. Remove from heat.

4. Dissolve miso in some of the broth, then return to the pot. Allow to steep briefly before serving.

Land and Sea Vegetable Salad

This combination of ingredients yields a highly nutritious salad with a tantalizing, somewhat exotic taste.

6-inch section wakame
Water for boiling wakame
1 bunch watercress (large stems removed), chopped
1 medium cucumber, quartered lengthwise, and sliced
1 head Boston (bibb) lettuce
2–3 radishes, trimmed and thinly sliced
2 tablespoons toasted sunflower or pumpkin seeds
Lemon-Tahini Dressing *(page 188)*

Serves: 4

1. Soak wakame in water to cover for 10 minutes, or until just tender. Rinse carefully to remove any shells clinging to the leaves.

2. Bring a small pot of water to a boil, and blanche wakame for a few seconds. Immediately plunge the fronds into cold water so they retain their color. Drain well, cut off and discard any tough ribs, chop fronds, and set aside in a medium-sized bowl.

3. Add watercress and cucumber to wakame and toss together. (Peel cucumber if waxed.)

4. Wash lettuce leaves and spin or pat dry.

5. Arrange bed of lettuce leaves on individual salad plates or in wide, shallow bowls. Place a mound of salad mixture on top of each serving. Edge each mound with radish slices and top with a sprinkling of roasted seeds.

6. Prepare dressing and serve on the side.

Vinegared Land and Sea Vegetables*

Cooling and colorful, this makes an appealing summer side dish.

Water for boiling vegetables
Pinch sea salt
1/2 cup thinly sliced carrot rounds
1/2 cup cauliflower florets
1/2 cup snow peas or sugar snap peas
1/2 cup bean sprouts
1/2 cup soaked, chopped wakame

DRESSING
4 tablespoons brown rice vinegar
1 tablespoon shoyu
1 tablespoon water

Serves: 3–4

1. Bring a pot of water to boil and add sea salt.

2. Boil carrots 2–3 minutes. Remove from pot, drain, and cool.

3. Boil cauliflower 3–4 minutes. Remove from pot, drain, and cool.

4. Boil peas 1–2 minutes. Remove, drain, and cool.

5. Boil bean sprouts 20–30 seconds. Remove, drain, and cool.

6. Boil wakame 10 seconds. Drain and immediately plunge into cold water to set color. Drain well and combine with other vegetables in serving bowl.

7. Mix dressing ingredients together, pour over vegetables, toss, and serve.

*Recipe from Peter and Montse Bradford, authors of *Cooking With Sea Vegetables.*

Lemon-Tahini Dressing

This simple dressing goes well with salads that feature flavor-intense vegetables such as watercress or dandelion. Lemon-Tahini Dressing goes exceptionally well on Land and Sea Vegetable Salad (page 186).

2 tablespoons tahini
1 tablespoon lemon juice
1 tablespoon mellow white miso
Water

Yield: About $\frac{1}{3}$ cup

1. In a small bowl, thoroughly combine first 3 ingredients.

2. Mix in water (tablespoon at a time) until desired consistency is achieved.

KANTEN

Kanten, known as agar-agar in the West, is an ancient vegetable gelatin traditionally made by freezing and drying extracts of various red sea vegetables. Kanten's natural jelling ability, mild flavor, and total lack of calories have made it a favorite with health-conscious cooks around the world. Kanten comes prepackaged in bars and flakes. Even without refrigeration, kanten sets quickly as it cools, and seals in the natural flavor and sweetness of any fruits and vegetables used. Light and refreshingly cool, kanten dishes are especially popular in the summer. In any season, kanten can be used with vegetables and stock to make molded aspics; as a substitute for pectin in jams, jellies, and cranberry sauce; and in desserts such as puddings and pie fillings.

MAKING TRADITIONAL SNOW-DRIED KANTEN

Today almost all kanten is made by a modern process. This procedure involves the use of sulfuric acid to dissolve the starches, and chemical bleaches and dyes to neutralize the color and flavor. However, a few small producers, such as the Mizoguchi family in the mountains of Nagano, Japan, still use the old labor-intense traditional method.

The natural snow-dried method begins on Japan's coast, where certain red sea vegetables of the *gelidium* species are harvested in the fall and sun-dried. The dried sea vegetables are bundled and taken up to the Mizoguchi shop to be made into kanten during the cold winter months.

Beginning in December, the sea vegetables are placed in a large cauldron with water and allowed to cook down for several hours. The resulting gel is allowed to cool. It is then cut into blocks, arranged on bamboo trays, and set outside on snow-covered rice paddies. Moisture in the gelatin freezes each night then thaws during the day. In about ten days, all the moisture is gone and the light, flaky bars of pure kanten remain. The crisp, porous, feather-light bars are then shaved into fine flakes and packaged.

COOKING WITH KANTEN

Naturally made snow-dried kanten is available in bars and flakes in most natural foods stores. The Mizoguchi family's kanten is sold in the United States under the Emerald Cove, Erewhon, Mitoku Macrobiotic, Sound Sea Vegetables, and Tree of

Life labels. A powdered variety is often sold in Oriental foods stores, but this type is usually made by the chemical process that is used in large factories. Read labels carefully and look for the words "snow-dried."

According to Peter and Montse Bradford, authors of *Cooking With Sea Vegetables*, the jelling ability of natural kanten varies according to the acidity or alkalinity of the food with which it is used. Acidic foods may require more kanten than alkaline foods do. Testing the recipe is recommended by taking a spoonful of the heated mixture and allowing it to rapidly set on a cool surface. If the mixture does not set in a few minutes, add a little more kanten to the pot and simmer a few more minutes.

To use kanten bars, tear them into several pieces and soak them in water for thirty to sixty minutes. Remove the kanten, squeeze out any excess water, and place in a saucepan along with the liquid called for in the recipe. The liquid should be cold or at room temperature. Bring to a simmer over medium heat without stirring. Once the liquid begins to simmer, stir occasionally until the kanten dissolves (about two to three minutes).

Prepackaged flakes need not be soaked. Simply sprinkle the measured amount over the liquid before heating and proceed as instructed for kanten bars. In any recipe, flakes can be substituted for bars and vice versa. The jelling strength of one bar of kanten is equal to two slightly rounded tablespoons of flakes.

KANTEN RECIPES

Apple-Sesame Custard*

Served chilled, Apple-Sesame Custard is a refreshing and satisfying summer dessert.

6 cups apple juice
1 cup kanten flakes
3 tablespoons finely grated lemon peel
Pinch sea salt
5 tablespoons sesame tahini
2 teaspoons vanilla

Serves: 6–8

1. Place apple juice, kanten flakes, lemon peel, and salt in a medium saucepan, and let soak for 10–15 minutes.

2. Bring juice mixture to a boil, lower heat, and simmer 3–5 minutes, stirring constantly until kanten flakes have completely dissolved. Remove from heat.

3. Place tahini in a small bowl. Gradually add $\frac{1}{3}$ cup of hot juice, stirring after each addition. When tahini reaches a thin, creamy consistency, add it to the pot along with vanilla. Stir.

4. Rinse a shallow bowl or casserole dish in water, then pour in the hot liquid. Leave to cool until firm.

5. Place mixture in a blender and purée until smooth. Return to serving bowl, chill, and serve either on its own or as a topping for other desserts.

*Recipe from Peter and Montse Bradford, authors of *Cooking With Sea Vegetables.*

Apple-Berry Cooler

Kanten makes an especially good summer dessert since it is light, cooling, and requires little time and heat to prepare.

4 cups juice (apple, apple-strawberry, or apple-raspberry)
Pinch sea salt
6 tablespoons kanten flakes
1 teaspoon finely grated lemon peel
1 teaspoon fresh lemon juice
2 cups fresh berries

Serves: 6

1. Pour juice into a saucepan and add salt. Sprinkle kanten over juice and allow to sit for 15 minutes.

2. Bring juice to a simmer over medium heat, stirring occasionally. Simmer 3 minutes, then remove from heat. Add lemon peel and juice.

3. Pour hot juice over fresh whole or sliced berries in a casserole dish or mold. Refrigerate or set in a cool place, uncovered. The kanten will be firm in 1–2 hours. (If you want kanten to set more quickly, place mixture in shallow individual serving bowls and refrigerate.)

14

BROWN RICE VINEGAR
Japan's Liquid Treasure

Since ancient times, people from all over the world have let "wild" acetic-acid bacteria turn their alcoholic beverages to vinegar. Each with its distinctive flavor, aroma, and color, "naturally-brewed" vinegars are derived from sugar cane, molasses, fruit, or grain. Vinegars are vital as food preservatives, and they play important roles in such products as health and beauty aids, antiseptics, cleaning solutions, and medicines. All vinegars share a mouth-puckering acidity that refreshes tired taste buds and stimulates the appetite.

One of the world's most nutritious and delicious vinegars is made from 100 percent brown rice wine (sake) that is fermented in earthenware crocks, which are buried in the ground. This unique 1,000-year-old method survives only on Japan's southern island of Kyushu. Because it is made from brown rice, with its bran and germ intact, *kuro-su* (black vinegar) has a high concentration of essential amino acids. It is recognized not only for its mellow taste but also for its medicinal quality.

Because it is rare and expensive, in Japan, Kyushu brown rice vinegar is usually taken as a health tonic. In the United States and Europe, it is sold in natural foods stores as a fine condiment.

Several brands of Kyushu-style brown rice vinegar sold in the United States are made by two companies, Maruboshi Vinegar Company and Date Shoten. Both companies are located in remote areas of Kyushu, away from industrial pollution. With pure water, mild climate, and abundant local rice, these companies enjoy ideal conditions for making brown rice vinegar.

MAKING BROWN RICE VINEGAR

At Maruboshi Vinegar Company, the vinegar-making process begins at local sake shops with a thick, primitive-type sake made from only two ingredients: brown rice and spring water. The sake-maker steams brown rice, sprinkles it with spores from an *Aspergillus* mold, and sets it to incubate in a warm, humid room. The spores germinate and the mold begins to produce digestive enzymes using the brown rice as a nutrient source. After two days, the fermented rice and *Aspergillus* mold becomes *koji* (the ubiquitous starter used in most Japanese fermented foods). The sake-maker next combines the koji with water and cooked brown rice, then pours the mixture into 100-gallon wooden casks.

Gradually, the enzymes in the koji convert the proteins, carbohydrates, and fats of the brown rice into simple amino acids, sweet sugars, and fatty acids. Next, naturally occurring yeast converts the sugars to ethyl alcohol.

After about eight weeks, the thick, heady brown rice sake automatically stops fermenting when its alcohol content reaches about 20 percent, which inhibits yeast growth. It is then delivered to the vinegar shop, where it is mixed with spring water and seed vinegar (good vinegar from a previous batch). Finally, the liquid is poured into partly buried crocks that are sealed with thick, natural-fiber paper and wooden or ceramic lids.

At Date Shoten, an even older, one-step method is used. The vinegar-makers combine the steamed brown rice, the koji, and well water directly in the crocks. Rather than add seed vinegar, the crock lids are briefly removed to allow wild acetic-acid bacteria to inoculate the mixture and work their magic to convert the sake to vinegar.

At both shops, the crocks, many over 100 years old, are arranged in rows going north to south; this is so each crock receives maximum warmth as the sun travels from east to west. In the summer, when warm temperatures could cause the vinegar to overheat, the grass is left to grow tall around the crocks to provide cooling shade.

In winter, the grass is cut short to expose the upper third of the crocks to the warming sun.

Within two to four months, depending on the season, the acetic-acid bacteria transforms the ethyl alcohol of the brown rice sake into dark, rich vinegar. The vinegar-maker pumps the vinegar from the crocks, dilutes it with water to reduce its acidity, and puts it in large tanks where it is left to age and mellow for about ten months. Once aged, the vinegar is filtered through cotton, flash-pasteurized, and bottled. The Kyushu vinegar process takes over a year to complete.

Kyushu brown rice vinegar is unique among natural rice vinegars because it is fermented outdoors. For centuries, Kyushu vinegar-makers have buried their brown, twenty-five gallon, glazed crocks about two-thirds in the ground. Maruboshi brewmaster Tetsunori Ezaki says, "This technique keeps the vinegar temperature constant over a narrow range. Daily and seasonal temperature fluctuations are very important because they give the vinegar deep character and richness, but," Ezaki warns, "temperature extremes can destroy the vinegar completely."

Authentic Kyushu brown rice vinegar accounts for less than 1 percent of Japan's annual 100-million-gallon vinegar production. During the Second World War, a shortage of rice encouraged the development of a much cheaper, quicker process. According to Togo Kuroiwa, author of *Rice Vinegar*, who spent most of his life trying to reestablish authentic rice-vinegar production in Japan, industrial rice-wine vinegar (sake "cake" vinegar) dates back to the early nineteenth century but became popular when the Japanese government rationed rice in 1942.

The quicker, industrial rice vinegar-making process does not use rice koji. Instead, it adds *sake lees*—the dregs left from sake manufacturing—to distilled grain alcohol. This mixture is fermented under controlled temperatures, and, in less than a month, bacteria convert the alcohol to acetic acid (distilled vinegar). Much more than flavor is lost in the sake lees-distilled alcohol process. Since the alcohol is distilled by boiling, most of the amino acids are left behind in the process. According to the Japan Food Research Laboratories, authentic rice vinegar has five times the amount of amino acids as sake-lees vinegar. What's more, it is the amino acids in vinegar that are most responsible for its medicinal powers (see *Vim and Vinegar*, page 198).

Vim and Vinegar

In his best-selling book Folk Medicine, Dr. D.C. Jarvis, an authority on old Vermont folk remedies, described an extraordinary experiment. He asked twenty-four people to keep a daily record of the food they ate for two years. They were to check the acid-alkaline reaction of their urine each day using a simple litmus-paper test. Comparing his patients' medical records with their urine tests, Jarvis saw a clear pattern. A few days before the onset of an illness, a patient's urine shifted from acid to alkaline. The alkaline reaction usually corresponded with eating specific foods. Jarvis was surprised to learn that one of Vermont's oldest and most popular tonic drinks, two teaspoons of apple cider vinegar and a teaspoon of honey in a cup of water, shifted the urine reaction back to a healthy acidic condition. Old timers, as Jarvis discovered, used vinegar for chronic fatigue, headache, high blood pressure, dizziness, sore throat, obesity, and a host of other ailments that afflicted both humans and farm animals.

Medical researchers now believe it is the amino acids present in vinegar that are partly responsible for its medicinal effects. In particular, these amino acids help counter the effects of lactic-acid buildup in the blood, which can cause fatigue; irritability; stiff, sore muscles; and can contribute to disease.

In Japan, scientific interest in authentic vinegar's health benefits is revitalizing the small Kyushu brown rice vinegar industry. Dr. Yoshio Takino of Shizuka University, Japan, has confirmed the importance of vinegar's amino acids. According to Takino, the twenty amino acids and sixteen organic acids found in authentic rice vinegar help prevent the formation of toxic fat peroxides. He explains that when unsaturated fatty acids from vegetable oils and other foods are heated and exposed to light in cooking or oxidized during metabolism, fat peroxides can form, which contribute to aging and to cholesterol formation on blood vessel walls.

However, for the stouthearted, the following old Japanese tonic is said to be very effective for increasing stamina and maintaining general *health. Wash an egg, being careful not to break the shell. Immerse the egg in a cup of brown rice vinegar for two to three days, or until the shell dissolves leaving the inner soft skin. Discard the skin and mix the egg and vinegar well. Drink a sake cup of this liquid three times a day (after meals). Known as* tamago-su *(egg-vinegar drink), this is one of Japan's most potent folk remedies.*

SHOPPING FOR BROWN RICE VINEGAR

When shopping for rice vinegar, read labels carefully. The highest-quality products are made from either brown rice or from a combination of sweet brown rice and water. Kyushu vinegar from Maruboshi Company and Date Shoten Company is imported to the United States in 55-gallon drums by Erewhon, Tree of Life, Granum (bottled as Mitoku Macrobiotic), and Great Eastern Sun (bottled as Mitoku Macrobiotic and Emperor's Kitchen). The price of this high-quality rice vinegar is lower in the United States than it is in Japan.

Although many Oriental foods store vinegars are half the price of natural foods brands, keep in mind that these lower-priced products are invariably made from distilled alcohol and sake lees. Some brands list wheat, rice, corn, sake lees, and alcohol as their ingredients, while other brands list no ingredients at all. It is impossible to judge the quality of rice vinegar by its color, since some Oriental food brands have added coloring agents.

Ironically, the finest brand Kyushu vinegars, such as Maruboshi and Date Shoten may contain a rice sediment, which, if disturbed, makes them look muddy. Rather then being a cause of concern, this sediment is a sign of quality.

COOKING WITH BROWN RICE VINEGAR

Refreshing and delicious, naturally brewed rice vinegar is a wonderful seasoning. Characterized by a light sweetness, it is full-bodied yet mild, without the sharpness often associated with industrial vinegar. You can enjoy brown rice vinegar in all the ways you enjoy other natural vinegars. A stimulating contrast of flavors, brown rice vinegar brings almost any food to life.

Besides being a mainstay in salad dressings, pickling mixtures, and marinades, rice vinegar also perks up sauces, dips, spreads, and entrées. Japanese housewives add a little rice vinegar to cooked summer rice to prevent it from spoiling. To make beans more digestible, add a little vinegar to the cooking liquid once the beans are tender. Brown rice vinegar also enhances the flavor of grain, vegetable, and fish dishes. It can help balance salt and fats, and reduce cravings for strong sweets.

BROWN RICE VINEGAR RECIPES

French Onion Dip

High in protein and low in calories, this versatile dip is great with a wide variety of snacks and appetizers.

8 ounces fresh tofu
3 level tablespoons mellow white miso
2 tablespoons brown rice vinegar
2 tablespoons sesame oil
1–2 cloves garlic, sliced
1 tablespoon rice malt
3 tablespoons minced fresh onion, or 2 tablespoons dried

Yield: 1 ½ cups

1. Place tofu in boiling water to cover. Turn off heat, cover, and let sit a few minutes. Remove tofu and cool briefly in cold water.

2. Crumble tofu into a blender along with all remaining ingredients except the onion. Blend until smooth. (It may be necessary to stop the blender and scrape down the sides with a spatula. If mixture is too thick, add a little water or plain soymilk.)

3. Stir in onion.

4. Refrigerate dip two hours to allow flavors to heighten.

5. Serve as a dip for chips or raw vegetables, or as a spread on crackers or rice cakes.

Cooking Chickpeas

The simple steps presented below should be followed when cooking dry chickpeas. Keep in mind: approximately ³⁄₄ cup of dry chickpeas becomes 2 cups when cooked.

1. *In a pot, soak dry chickpeas 8–12 hours (or boil 5 minutes and soak 2 hours), then drain.*
2. *Cover drained beans with an inch or two of fresh water and bring to a boil. Reduce heat and simmer until beans are just tender, adding water as needed to keep beans covered.*
3. *Add ¹⁄₂ teaspoon sea salt per cup of dry beans used, and simmer another 15 minutes.*
4. *Drain and cool.*

Cooked chickpeas will keep up to a week in the refrigerator. They are a welcome addition to pasta dishes, grain and vegetable salads, marinated vegetables, sautéed greens, soups, and casseroles.

Chickpea Salad

Marinated Chickpea Salad, *though light enough for the warmest spring and summer days, is no nutritional lightweight. The combination of chickpeas and broccoli makes this a nutritional dish, especially rich in protein, calcium, and iron.*

2 cups cooked chickpeas (see Cooking Chickpeas, *page 202)*

2 tablespoons extra virgin olive oil

1 tablespoon freshly squeezed lemon juice

2 tablespoons brown rice vinegar

1 clove garlic, finely minced or pressed

Sea salt, to taste

Pepper, to taste (optional)

1 cup small parboiled broccoli florets, drained and cooled

½ small red or white onion, diced

2–3 tablespoons minced fresh parsley

1 tablespoon minced fresh basil, mint, or dill (optional)

Serves: 4–5

1. In a small bowl, combine oil, lemon, vinegar, garlic, salt, and pepper. Mix well.

2. In another bowl, toss beans, broccoli, onion, parsley, and herbs together. Pour dressing over bean mixture and toss.

3. Let sit at least 30 minutes before serving. Stir occasionally to marinate evenly. Stored in a covered jar or bowl in the refrigerator, this salad will be at its best a day or two after it is made.

4. To serve, line small bowls with leaf lettuce, fill with marinated bean mixture, and garnish with parsley or sprig of whichever herb is used in the salad.

Tofu-Sesame Dressing

This dressing is delicious on tossed or pressed salads and is a favorite on hijiki or arame salads.

4 ounces fresh tofu
$\frac{1}{4}$ cup light sesame, canola, or safflower oil
1 $\frac{1}{2}$–2 teaspoons toasted sesame oil
2 $\frac{1}{2}$ tablespoons brown rice vinegar
$\frac{1}{4}$ cup water
3 tablespoons mellow miso
1 clove garlic
1 tablespoon rice malt
1 tablespoon sesame seeds

Yield: Approximately 1$\frac{1}{2}$ cups

1. Place tofu in a pot, cover with water, and boil 1 minute. Turn off heat and let tofu sit a few minutes. Remove tofu and cool briefly in cold water.

2. Crumble tofu into a blender or suribachi along with all remaining ingredients except sesame seeds. Blend or mix until smooth.

3. Toast seeds in a dry skillet by stirring constantly over medium heat for 2–3 minutes.

4. Pour dressing into a bowl, mix in seeds, and chill slightly before serving.

Marinated Tofu and Scallions

This dish is very quick and easy to prepare, but it must be started about 1 ½ hours before mealtime so the tofu will have a chance to absorb the flavor of the marinade.

1 block fresh tofu (approximately 1 pound)
¾ cup scallions, cut on the diagonal into ½-inch lengths

MARINADE
1 ½ cups water or mild-flavored vegetable stock
¼ cup shoyu or 3 tablespoons tamari
2 tablespoons mirin
2 tablespoons brown rice vinegar
3 small cloves garlic, pressed or finely minced
2 teaspoons peeled and finely grated ginger
1 teaspoon dried tarragon (optional)

Serves: 4

1. Combine all marinade ingredients in a medium-sized bowl.

2. Cut tofu crosswise into ½-inch-thick slices, then cut the slices into 1 x 1 ½-inch pieces. Wrap tofu pieces in a cheesecloth or clean kitchen towel and pat gently to remove excess water. Place tofu in the marinade, and let sit at least 1 hour.

3. Remove tofu from marinade and arrange in single layer in a large skillet. Add about ⅓ inch of marinade to the pan. (If desired, strain out garlic from marinade.) Cover and bring to a boil, then lower heat and simmer gently 5 minutes.

4. Sprinkle scallions over tofu, cover, and cook 3 minutes more. Serve hot.

Amazake Salad Dressing

This creamy, slightly sweet yet tart dressing is terrific on all types of salads.

$\frac{1}{2}$ *cup amazake*
2 tablespoons light sesame oil
2 tablespoons extra virgin olive oil
$\frac{1}{4}$ *cup brown rice vinegar*
1 tablespoon red (rice) miso
1 clove garlic, sliced

Yield: 1 cup

1. Blend all ingredients in a blender until smooth.

2. Serve on vegetable, grain, and pasta salads.

15

TRADITIONAL VESSELS
Vats, Crocks, and Barrels

Making food in small batches by hand requires years of experience and good intuition. Traditional equipment helps insure that the final product will have authentic flavor and texture.

The hallmark of traditional Japanese fermented foods is that they are usually made in wooden or ceramic vessels. After centuries of fermenting miso, soy sauce, sake, vinegar, umeboshi, pickles, and mirin in cedar vats or ceramic crocks, old brewmasters refuse to use modern substitutes. They claim traditional vessels give their products a depth of character and complexity that is impossible to achieve with plastic and stainless steel.

During our trip to Japan, while working with Mitoku Company's miso-maker Takamichi Onozaki, one of John's responsibilities was to climb down into an empty eight-foot-deep, seven-foot-wide cedar miso vat to scrub the inside walls clean with hot water and salt, using a bamboo brush. As he worked, paying particular attention to cracks and crevices in the old wood, the heady aroma of miso and cedar filled the air. The experience left him convinced that food fermented in cedar vats must be qualitatively different from food made in plastic or stainless steel tanks.

According to miso-master Onozaki, wooden vats allow fermenting food to breathe. Air passes through the wood to mellow and darken the food within. This aging process is the same method still used by high-quality wine makers.

In addition, substances that form during fermentation, such as alcohols, can actually dissolve natural tannins in the wood that flavor the food. The newer the wood and the higher the alcohol content of the ingredients, the more tannin enters the food.

The complex biochemical process of food fermentation is directly affected by the many different strains and varieties of microorganisms present. To help maintain the characteristic qualities of foods fermented in a particular shop or region, some brewers inoculate each new batch of food with some of their mature product. Others, such as Onozaki, rely on the myriad microorganisms in the wood of their old vats to serve the same purpose. After decades or even centuries of association with a particular company's foods, these organisms are always present to begin new fermentations year after year.

Although wooden vats are cleaned after each fermentation, unlike plastic and stainless steel tanks, it is impossible to sterilize them with heat and cleansers. Ironically, overcleaning fermentation vessels may reduce the food value of the final product. Because yeast cells synthesize proteins and vitamins (especially B vitamins) as they grow, they actually make food more nutritious than it was before fermentation. Overcleaning fermentation tanks, particularly with steam heat and strong soaps, greatly reduces the diversity of fermenting organisms. Tests have shown a greater diversity of beneficial microorganisms present in foods aged in wood compared to foods made in synthetic tanks.

Also, compared to modern materials, wood is an excellent insulator. The thick wooden stays of large vats protect the fermenting food from the extremes of hot and cold. Wide swings in temperature during fermentation not only affect the taste of the finished product by altering the metabolism of fermenting organisms, but can totally destroy a batch of soy sauce, miso, or sake.

It is not just wooden vats that work their magic on fermenting foods. Tetsunori Ezaki, maker of Mitoku Organic Kyushu Brown Rice Vinegar, says that only ceramic crocks make mellow, delicious Kyushu vinegar. When Ezaki experimented with stainless steel and plastic tanks, the vinegar overheated resulting in incomplete fermentation.

Before the advent of modern technology and materials, the making of traditional vessels for fermenting food was a highly respected art requiring great skill and experience. In Japan, wooden vats of all sizes are made by special carpenters called *okeyasan* (*oke* means barrel or vat). Today, okeyasan rarely make new large cedar vats like the ones used by Mitoku's food producers, but they are often called upon to repair or recondition old vats that are leaking or in need of new bamboo hoops. Okeyasan also keep busy by making small cedar pickle barrels for home use. Many Japanese housewives who take pride in their homemade pickles insist on using only wooden barrels.

THE MASTER OF HOOPS

During our stay in Japan, while working at the Onozaki shop, John had the rare experience of helping Haru Arai—one of Japan's last okeyasan—repair three huge cedar vats. John recounts:

> Even before meeting him, we knew him well: "the okeyasan." A household word, it elicited smiles at its mere utterance. Haru Arai came early one crisp fall morning with a big bag of tools on his back. He was riding a large black bike, which seemed two sizes too big for him. We were eating breakfast on the front porch. The okeyasan slid open the porch door and walked in, while repeating the words "good morning" and bowing as he walked. Although his entrance was casual, everyone stopped eating and bowed their heads low. He was very small, under five feet tall and about eighty pounds, with gentle black eyes and short silver hair. He was dressed in a traditional thick cotton vest and baggy pants drawn to the calves by black boots with a split for his big toe.
>
> Arai-san (his family name) was a local legend as master cooper (barrel maker), herbal doctor, folk singer, and the best talker in the community. Having spent the last fifty-eight years foraging the forest for the bamboo and wood that he used in his work, Arai-san had become an authority on the location and uses of herbs and wild foods. In the seven months we spent studying fermented foods in the village of Shimo Isano, north of Tokyo, we met many of these hardy oldsters. However, Arai-san was exceptional; his skill, strength, and wittiness are rare at any age.

Japanese old-timers are strong, traditional, often independent people. Although urban Japan is rapidly becoming a model of a technological society, rural Japan is changing more slowly. The lifestyle, particularly of the older people, is still very traditional, centered around the extended family. Daily responsibilities are shared and usually focus on basic needs.

In such a community, old people have much to do and are highly respected. Having lived long, productive lives, they are experienced in such varied subjects as language, history, medicinal foods and herbs, cooking, building, and child care. In addition, they usually have a better sense for predicting the weather than modern meteorological equipment.

> The okeyasan worked with deep concentration, his existence focused on the task at hand. Even though his hearing was excellent, he had to be called several times for tea breaks and lunch (although the sound of a young lady's voice readily got his attention).
>
> Arai-san ate a traditional diet of rice, miso soup, pickles, vegetables, and very salty fish. He ate slowly and in very small quantities. This simple diet, along with working hard each day, seems to have given him a strong constitution that is serving him well in old age.

The special art of the okeyasan is the transformation of cedar trees into barrels and vats. His work is a combination of wood sculpturing and bamboo braiding. The curved wooden barrel staves are usually held together with braided bamboo hoops, rather than hoops made of iron. This is due to the incompatibility of the iron and the salt used in food fermentation.

Arai-san had been making wooden barrels for fifty-eight years. Starting as a helper when he was thirteen years old, he worked with his uncle making large wooden vats for sake. His first responsibilities were carrying wood and sharpening tools. As a young man he was head okeyasan at a large sake brewery. Under his direction, a crew of five men worked for days using special tools and skills to make the vats. However, with the advent of steel technology, these were replaced by stainless steel containers.

Due to the high cost of good wood, labor, and the scarcity of okeyasans, new wooden barrels are expensive. However, most families have a few old barrels handed down from their ancestors. Although few people have a technical understanding of fermentation, they have the practical knowledge that miso, shoyu, and pickles fermented in wooden barrels taste better than those fermented in plastic, steel, or glass containers. In the Japanese countryside, older people still understand the superior quality of food fermented in wooden barrels, so the okeyasan is very busy. Often, he works on Sundays and holidays, crafting things from two-gallon pickle barrels to fifteen-foot-tall shoyu vats.

John will always remember his unique experience with Arai-san:

> Mr. Onozaki, our miso master, needed to replace the bamboo hoops on three of his miso vats. I was chosen to help the okeyasan. Like most older Japanese people, Arai-san used a local dialect, which was hard for us to understand. However, it soon became apparent that it was faith, more than linguistic understanding, that I was going to need.
>
> The following morning, Arai-san and I climbed the mountain behind the house. Spotting a large bamboo shaft, he drew his axe and felled it with

The okeyasan hammers the bamboo hoop until it fits tightly around the barrel.

three powerful blows. I stepped to the side as the thirty-foot, hundred-pound shaft crashed to the forest floor. I reached for the heavy end, but, in a flash, Arai-san already had the tree balanced on his shoulder and had started down the steep mountain. Except for his gray hair and weathered hands, he looked, at seventy-one years old, like a young boy.

The okeyasan spent many days working alone. Using simple hand tools, he would often spit on his hands for lubrication. Working with the natural flow of energy, he split large bamboo trees lengthwise into many strips. With concentrated movements, using leverage and gravity, he braided the strips into hoops that were about ten inches wide and weighed about forty pounds. Each hoop took nearly four hours to make; each vat needed seven hoops.

With the help of five or six other people, we turned the first vat upside down. Arai-san tossed the first hoop over the vat, threw some tools on top, climbed up, and signaled me to follow. Finally, it was time to help. I listened to my instructions in disbelief. Hanging over the side of the seven-foot-tall vat, I was to hold a short-handled wooden mallet on the upper edge of the bamboo hoop while the okeyasan, standing over me, swung a twenty-five-pound wooden mallet down to hit the small mallet I held in my hand. By moving the small mallet a few inches after each blow, the hoop would be driven down tightly around the vat. The responsibility of holding the small mallet on the edge of the hoop at just the right angle weighed heavily on my mind. A miss would, at best, damage the hoop; at worst, smash my hand and cause the okeyasan to fall to the ground below. The prospect of swinging the big mallet myself did not seem any more inviting.

I held my breath as the big mallet flew past my head when the okeyasan struck the first blow. It was a direct hit. I moved the mallet to the next position. About a hundred direct hits later, the first hoop was in place. By the third hoop, I felt confident enough to use two mallets, like drumsticks, to beat out the okeyasan's rhythm as he worked; by the fifth hoop, I was swinging the big mallet myself. Many days and several thousand hits later, the three vats were ready for miso. My hand was spared, and only one hoop was partially damaged.

It was weeks later that I discovered the okeyasan's eyes were less than perfect. I showed him a picture of himself, which he studied for quite a time and seemed to enjoy. However, the next person he passed it to laughed hysterically—the picture was upside down. It was fifty years of experience, rather than 20/20 vision, that guided the okeyasan's big hammer.

The okeyasan did not work on large vats often, so he had to make many of the special tools he needed for such work. More often he makes pickle barrels. Using special hand-planes and knives, flat pieces of wood are cut and planed into curved staves. These are glued together with rice paste and held in place with braided bamboo hoops. Finally, three or four planks are glued together and cut into a round piece to be used for a bottom. This bottom piece is pounded and glued into place. With care these pickle barrels can last two hundred years.

Each day after work, Arai-san sharpened his wit with sake, and we all gathered around for the show. He became a commentator rather than a storyteller. He was able to transform another person's simple statement into an exciting commentary annotated with details from seventy years of country life. It didn't take much to get him to laugh. My wife, Jan, and I had only to speak simple Japanese, country-style, and he would throw back his head and laugh with his whole body. Soon we learned which words he liked to hear and used them just to watch his hilarious reaction. Finally, from a mixture of intoxication and exhaustion from laughing, the okeyasan would make his exit, riding off into the cold night on his bike.

Arai-san had been drinking every night for twenty years. He believed that sake is a medicine that, in moderation, contributes to long life. He drank two full water glasses each night. We often joked about his "moderation."

Each morning, I half-expected to find him holding his head, but there he would be, out on the porch getting ready to start work.

From months spent working, eating, talking, and drinking with Arai-san, one lesson had become clear: Tradition, for Arai-san, is not an option but a very basic necessity of life. It is almost as biological as chromosomal DNA. Tradition for him carries a kind of genetic code for cultural stability and personal happiness. The rhythm of Arai-san's everyday life is guided by centuries of cultural experience. He does not experience his life as a fleeting moment in time but rather as part of his ancestral stream flowing out of ancient history.

As a gift from Arai-san and his ancestors, he made us three small pickle barrels of the highest-quality cedar. He worked on them for more than a week, carving, gluing, and braiding. On the bottom of one of the barrels, using permanent ink, he wrote a short story in thick, black Chinese characters. We still don't understand completely the meaning of all the characters, but there is no hurry—the barrels will be around well into the next century.

Just before we returned to the United States, the okeyasan showed us how to make *doboroku* (homemade sake). A master brewer, his doboroku, made from fermented rice and water, fueled our imaginations and warmed our bodies on many winter nights.

One day soon we will attempt to make a batch of the okeyasan's doboroku. If it turns out well, we'll drink a toast to old Arai-san, his work, and his traditional way of life.

Glossary

Amazake (rice milk). A sweetener or refreshing drink made from cooked sweet rice and koji starter that has fermented into a thick liquid. Also spelled amasake.

Arame. A mild-tasting sea vegetable that is similar to hijiki. Arame is a brown algae that grows in deep waters. Rich in iron, calcium, and other minerals, arame is often cooked with sweet root vegetables and served as a side dish.

Aspergillus. A specific group of molds used to inoculate beans and grains to make koji, *Aspergillus* is the starter for many Japanese fermented foods.

Azuki beans. Small, dark red beans. Especially good when cooked with kombu and winter squash. This bean is also spelled adzuki or aduki.

Bancha tea. Japan's coarse summer tea leaves that are sold as lower-quality green tea.

Bifun noodles. Light, transparent noodles made from rice flour and potato starch.

Burdock. A hardy plant that grows wild and is cultivated throughout the United States, as well as in Japan. The long, dark burdock root is delicious in soups, stews, and vegetable dishes. It is highly valued in macrobiotic diets for its strengthening qualities. Burdock's Japanese name is *gobo*.

Cha. The Japanese word for tea.

Cha-no-yu. The Zen Buddhist tea ceremony.

Couscous. Partly refined, cracked wheat.

Daikon. A long, white radish. Daikon helps dissolve stagnant fat deposits that have accumulated in the body. Freshly grated raw daikon is especially helpful in the digestion of oily foods.

Dashi. An all-purpose stock usually made with kombu and flavored with dried shiitake or bonito flakes.

Eritadenine. A substance found in shiitake that lowers blood cholesterol.

Fu. A dried wheat-gluten product. Available in thin sheets or thick round cakes, fu is a satisfying high-protein food used in soups, stews, and vegetable dishes.

Gyokuro. Japan's rarest, most expensive tea, Gyokuro is made from the tender first tea leaves of spring.

Hijiki. A dark brown sea vegetable that turns black when dried, hijiki has a spaghetti-like consistency. It is stronger-tasting than arame and is very high in calcium, iron, and protein. Also spelled hiziki.

Hojicha tea. A Japanese tea made from roasted coarse leaves and stems.

Kaiseki. A traditional Japanese meal consisting of a series of small, seasonal dishes, each resembling an appetizer both in size and beauty of presentation. Natural, hand-crafted serving ware is carefully chosen to complement the season, the food, and the food's arrangement. Like the tea ceremony, kaiseki was initially a formal, highly refined, spiritual discipline marked by the Zen ideals of simplicity, harmony, and restraint.

Kata dofu. A firm, coarse type of tofu.

Koji. Grains or beans inoculated with *Aspergillus* mold and used as a starter for most Japanese fermented foods, including miso, tamari, shoyu, amazake, mirin, and rice vinegar.

Kombu. A wide, thick, dark green sea vegetable that is rich in minerals. Kombu is often cooked with beans and vegetables. A single piece may be used two or three times to flavor a soup stock.

Kori dofu. Tofu that has been dehydrated by a natural freezing and drying process. Also called snow-dried tofu.

Koya dofu. A form of snow-dried tofu that has been dehydrated in a heated shed.

Kukicha tea. A Japanese tea made from roasted tea twigs and stems.

Kuro-su. The Japanese name for brown rice vinegar. Kuro-su is valued for its high concentration of essential amino acids, its medicinal qualities, and its mellow taste.

Kuzu. A white starch made from the root of the wild kuzu plant. In the United States, the plant densely populates the southern states, where it is known as kudzu. It is used in making soups, sauces, desserts, and medicinal beverages.

Matcha. The jade green powdered tea used in the Japanese tea ceremony.

Mirin. Sweet rice wine traditionally made by a complex distillation and double-fermentation process. Used in cooking as a high-quality sweetener and seasoning.

Miso. A protein-rich, fermented bean paste made from soybeans, usually with the addition of barley or brown or white rice. Miso is used in soup stocks and as a seasoning. When consumed on a regular basis, it aids circulation and digestion.

Mizu ame (sweet water). *See* Rice malt.

Mochi. A heavy rice cake or dumpling made from cooked, pounded sweet rice. Mochi is especially good for lactating mothers, as it promotes the production of breast milk. Mochi can be made at home or purchased ready-made.

Moromi. The thick slurry of fermenting koji and other ingredients that forms during the brewing process of soy sauce, sake, and mirin.

Mugwort. A mineral-rich herb that is dried and used as a medicinal tea. Dried, ground mugwort is also added to mochi and soba noodles.

Muro. A uniquely constructed room used to incubate koji.

Nature farming. A type of organic agriculture that originated in Japan.

Nigari. The traditional Japanese tofu coagulant, nigari is extracted from dehydrated sea water.

Nori. Thin sheets of dried sea vegetable. Nori is often roasted over a flame until its color turns from black or purple to green. It is used as a garnish, wrapped around rice balls or other foods, or cooked with tamari as a condiment. Rich in vitamin A and protein, nori also contains calcium, iron, and vitamins B1, B2, C, and D.

O-cha. The Japanese word for tea, o-cha is also used to designate a tea break.

O-hagi. Mochi that has been formed into small flat cakes or balls, then coated with puréed azuki beans or chestnuts, roasted and ground nuts or sesame seeds, or soybean flour.

Okeyasan. Name for Japanese carpenters who specialize in making and repairing traditional wooden vats and barrels.

O-toso. A medicinal drink made by infusing a combination of herbs in mirin. O-toso is traditionally drunk on New Year's day.

Rice malt. A natural, high-quality sweetener made from malted barley or koji, rice, and water.

Sake. Fermented rice wine made from koji and rice. Sake is usually served warm in small cups but can be served at room temperature or chilled. Also used as a seasoning in Oriental cooking.

Sashimi. Raw, slivered fish, usually served with a dip made of shoyu and wasabi.

Sencha. High-quality Japanese green tea made from young, tender leaves.

Shiitake. Cultivated medicinal mushrooms grown on hardwood logs or enriched sawdust.

Shochu. A concentrated distilled alcoholic drink.

Shoyu. Fermented soy sauce made with cultured wheat and soybeans, water, and sea salt.

Soba. Noodles made from buckwheat flour or a combination of buckwheat and wheat flour. Some varieties contain other ingredients such as dried mugwort powder, mountain yam flour, or powdered green tea.

Somen. Very thin Japanese wheat noodles.

Suribachi. A special serrated, glazed clay bowl. Used with a pestle—called a surikogi—the suribachi is used for grinding and puréeing foods. An essential item in the macrobiotic kitchen, the suribachi can be used in a variety of ways to make condiments, spreads, dressings, baby foods, nut butters, and medicinal preparations.

Sushi. Vinegared rice that is rolled with vegetables, fish, or pickles, then wrapped in nori, and sliced into rounds. The most healthful sushi is made with brown rice and other natural ingredients.

Tahini. A nut butter that is obtained by grinding white sesame seeds until smooth and creamy. It is used like sesame butter.

Tamago-su (egg vinegar). A medicinal tonic made by dissolving an egg in rice vinegar.

Tamari. A wheat-free fermented soy sauce made with cultured soybeans, water, and sea salt.

Tempura. A method of cooking in which vegetables, fish, or seafood are coated with batter and deep-fried in vegetable oil. Tempura is often served with soup, rice or noodles, and pickles.

Te-uchi. Hand-made Japanese noodles.

Tofu. Soybean curd made from soybeans and nigari. Used in soups, vegetable dishes, dressings, etc., tofu is high in protein, low in fat, and cholesterol-free. *See also* Kori-dofu.

Udon. Japanese noodles made from wheat, whole wheat, or whole wheat and unbleached flour.

Umeboshi. Tart, salty Japanese pickled plums, which stimulate the appetite and digestion, and aid in maintaining an alkaline blood quality. Shiso leaves impart a reddish color and natural flavoring to the plums during pickling. Umeboshi can be used whole or in the form of paste.

Wakame. A long, thin brown sea vegetable used in a variety of dishes. High in protein, iron, and manganese, wakame has a sweet taste and a delicate texture. It is especially good in miso soup.

Wasabi. A light green Japanese root that has been dried, powdered, and made into a paste. It is traditionally used as a seasoning in sushi, sashimi, and in dipping sauces. Wasabi is very hot with a taste reminiscent of horseradish.

Worldwide
Importers

The following companies import Mitoku products. Unless otherwise noted, the brand name is the same as the company name. If you are unable to find these products, ask your natural foods store to contact importers in your area.

Australia

Pureharvest
Attn: Mr. Don Lazzaro and
  Mr. Daniel Hannaford
PO Box 187
East Bentleigh, Victoria 3165
Tel: 61-3-579-3422

Austria

Lebenszeichen
Attn: Mr. Hans Daurer

Grosshart 99
8272 Grosshart
Austria
Tel: 43-3333-2833

Naturgarten
Attn: Mr. Gert Pierer
A-8462 Gamlitz 254
Austria
Tel: 43-3453-4846-0

Belgium

Lima N.V.
Attn: Mr. Mark Callebert
Edgar Gevaertdreef 10
B-9830 St. Martens-Latem
Belgium
Tel: 32-91-82-42-76

Canada

Koyo Foods, Inc.
Attn: Mr. Tosh Kagemori
393 Boulevard Ste-Croix, Suite A
St. Laurent, Quebec H4N 2L3
Tel: 514-744-1299

Costa Rica

Distribuidora De Productos Macrobi-
  oticos S.A.
Attn: Mr. Roberto Gutierrez
PO Box 7785-1000
San Jose, Costa Rica
Tel: 506-279584

Czechoslovakia

Sunfood Company
Attn: Mr. Mervart Vaclav
Jiráskova 557
518 01 Dobruska
Czechoslovakia
Tel: 42-443-21817

Denmark

Grøn Distribution APS
Attn: Mr. Thomas Anderson
Høje Gladsaxe Torv 2
2860 Søborg, Denmark
Tel: 45-31-67-41-90

England

Clearspring, Ltd.
Attn: Mr. Jonathan Toase
Unit 19A Acton Park Estate
London W3 7QE, England
Tel: 44-81-749-1781

Finland

Oy MakroBios Ab
Attn: Mr. Henrik Nyberg
Leksvall
SF-10600 Ekenäs, Finland
Tel: 358-11-204446

France

Tama
Attn: Mr. Noboru Sakaguchi
883 Rue De Bernau
94500 Champigny-Sur-Marne, France
Tel: 33-1-4983-7994

Celnat
Attn: Mr. Jean Celle
Z.I. Blavozy-St. Germain
43700 Brives-Charensac, France
Tel: 33-71-03-04-14

Germany

Biogarten
Attn: Mrs. Roswitha Weber
Gartenweg 2
8011 Anzing-Neufarn, Germany
Tel: 49-89-900005-0
Brand name: *Arche*

Greece

Diavgeia
Attn: Mr. Nicholas Linardatos
8 Feron Street
104 34 Athens, Greece
Tel: 30-1-88-30-602

Israel

Tivoli Natural Products, Ltd.
Attn: Batya Farhi
PO Box 28157
Tel-Aviv 61281 Israel
Tel: 972-3-377222

Italy

La Finestra Sul Cielo SRL
Attn: Mr. Adriano Poggio
Via Brandizzo 149
10088 Volpiano (TO), Italy
Tel: 39-11-995-1818

KI SRL
Attn: Mr. Roberto Durante
Via C. Marchesi 9
10093 Collegno (To), Italy
Tel: 39-11-720-654

Probios SRL
Attn: Mr. Fernando Favilli
Via Ponte de Mezzo 54
50127 Firenze, Italy
Tel: 39-55-352820

Dalla Terra Al Cielo
Attn: Mrs. Anna Maria Carboni
Via Cenni 17
10095 Grugliasco (TO), Italy
Tel: 39-11-4111-851

Solo Natura SRL
Attn: Mr. Borella
Via Campagnazza, 3
42027 Montecchio Emilia (RE), Italy
Tel: 39-522-865500

Netherlands

Fertilia B.V.
Attn: Mr. Dirk Jan Limburg
PO Box 447
8200 AK
Lelystad, Netherlands
Tel: 31-3200-80100
Brand name: *Hofu*

New Zealand

Austin Holdings
Attn: Mr. Austin Holden
CPO Box 3007
Aukland 1, New Zealand
Tel: 64-9-276-9691
Brand names: *Kaiora Natural, Mitoku Macrobiotic*

Enso International (NZ), Ltd.
Attn: Jon and Iko Judson
PO Box 1233
228 Antigua Street
Christchurch, New Zealand
Tel: 64-3-653-654

Healtheries of New Zealand, Ltd.
Attn: Mr. Mark Mathews
PO Box 11-201
Ellerslie
Auckland, New Zealand
Tel: 64-9-5793-179

Norway

Alternative Mat A/S avd. Import
Attn: Mr. Thomas Dyrnes
Box 2136
Grunerløkka
0505 Oslo 5, Norway
Tel: 47-2-373354

Poland

Firma Handlowa "Arame"
Attn: Mr. Bozena Ryszawska
Ul. Zmudzka 3/1
51-315 Wroclaw, Poland
Tel: 48-71-241247

Portugal

J.L. Ferreira, LDA
Attn: Mr. Manuel Martins
Parada Do
Alto S, Jodo, 17-A
1900 Lisboa, Portugal
Tel: 351-1-837673

Singapore

Nature's Best Pte., Ltd.
Attn: Mrs. Jackie Park-See
Blk 203 Henderson Industrial Park
Henderson Road #03-08
Singapore 0316
Tel: 65-2789978

South Africa, Republic of

Key Health
Attn: Mrs. Noeleen Cohen
39 Athlone Road
Parkview 2193, Johannesburg
Republic of South Africa
Tel: 27-11-646-9797

Spain

Kunga, C.B.
Attn: Mr. Juan Rubio
Pza, Nueva 17
Alicante 03001, Spain
Tel: 34-6-520-8600

Sweden

Kung Markatta
Attn: Mr. Lennart Olsson
Hjälmarsberg
S-705 95 Örebro, Sweden
Tel: 46-19-32-11-90

Switzerland

S'Lotus Bluemli
Attn: Mr. Martin Burkard
Gewerbestrasse 10B
CH-4552 Derendingen, Switzerland
Tel: 41-65-42-13-42

Terrasana AG
Attn: Bruno and Maya Thurig
Römerweg 19
CH-8307 Effretikon, Switzerland
Tel: 41-52-32-54-20

United States

Granum, Inc.
Attn: Mr. Blake Rankin
2901 N.E. Blakeley Street
Seattle, WA 98105
Tel: (206) 525-0051
Brand names: *Mitoku Macrobiotic,
Choice, Kaiseki Select, Sound Sea Vegetables*

Great Eastern Sun
Attn: Mr. Don DeBona
92 McIntosh Road
Asheville, NC 28806
Tel: (704) 252-3090
Brand names: *Mitoku Macrobiotic, Emerald Cove, Emperor's Kitchen, Haiku, Macro Pasta*

Macrobiotic Wholesale Company
Attn: Kurt and Else Schmitz
799 Old Leicester Highway
Asheville, NC 28806
Tel: (704) 252-1221
Brand name: *Mitoku Macrobiotic*

Shojin/Golden Son
Attn: Mr. Bhagavan Buritz
PO Box 247
Kealakekua, HI 96750
Tel: (808) 322-3651
Brand name: *Mitoku Macrobiotic*

Tree of Life
Attn: Dot Peck
PO Box 410
St. Augustine, FL 32085
Tel: (904) 825-2042
Brand names: *Mitoku Macrobiotic, Tree of Life*

U.S. Mills, Inc.
Attn: Mr. Charles Verde
395 Elliot Street
Newton Upper Falls, MA 02164
Tel: (617) 969-5400
Brand name: *Erewhon*

Westbrae Natural Foods
Attn: Ms. Lynne Minsky
1065 East Walnut Street
Carson, CA 90746
Tel: (310) 886-8200
Brand names: *Westbrae, Soba Shop*

Index